해석은 되는데 무슨 말인지 모르겠어요.

* 단어만 안다고 해석이 되는 것이 아니고
  해석이 된다고 문장의 의미가 모두 파악되는 것도 아닙니다.

누구나 다 겪어 보는 상황들

1. 어디서부터 해석을 해야 하는지 난감 하네!
2. 주어가 뭐지, 아니 어디까지가 주어지?
3. 동사는 도대체 어디 있는 건가?

다음 문장 해석 해 보기!

The man found dead in the alley had no family to contact with.

다음 문장 의미 파악하기, 주어 찾기

Keeping good ideas floating around in your head is a great way to ensure that they won't happen.

책을 출간하면서

일반적으로 독해를 하는데 가장 중요한 부분은 어휘력입니다. 단어를 알지 못하면 두말 할 것도 없이 문장을 이해할 수 없습니다. 어휘력을 갖춘 상태에서 문장을 이해하려면 어느 정도 문법 실력이 필요합니다. 그리고 우리의 영어 교육과정이 대부분 독해력, 즉 학생들의 문장 이해 능력을 묻는 과정이므로 영어 문장에 대한 이해력을 향상시키기 위해서는 다양한 문장을 경험 해 보는 것이 필수적입니다.

그래서 제가 28년 동안 학생들을 가르치면서 학생들이 해석하고 이해하는 데 어려움을 겪는 문장 형태를 파악하여, 문장 하나하나를 찾고, 만들어서 제작하게 되었습니다.

"딱 한권으로 정리되는 구문독해"의 가장 큰 장점은 앞서 말씀 드린바와 같이 학생들을 직접 가르쳐 왔고, 현재도 가르치고 있는 샘이 제작했다는 것입니다.

저자 **안 천 구**

네이버에서 검색해 보세요~

Contents...

Chapter 1
- Part 1. 형식에 관한 문장 .... 8 ~ 19
  - Exercise (1~4)
- Part 2. 나는 주어다!!! .... 20 ~ 37
  - Check Point (1, 2, 3)
- Part 3. 보어는 주어 혹은 목적어를 보충 설명 .... 38 ~ 46
  - Check Point (4)
  - Stop (1) 모르면 해석이 안 되는 필수 구문
- Part 4. 목적어가 필요해! .... 47 ~ 58
  - Check Point (5, 6)
  - Stop (2) 모르면 해석이 안 되는 대동사
  - Stop (3) 모르면 해석이 안 되는 대명사

Chapter 2
- Part 1. 동사 .... 60 ~ 66
  - Check Point (7)
- Part 2. 조동사 .... 67 ~ 76
  - Check Point (8, 9)
- Part 3. 수동태 .... 77 ~ 85
  - Check Point (10)
- Part 4. 가정법 .... 86 ~ 93
  - Check Point (11)
  - Stop (4) 모르면 해석이 안 되는 필수 어휘

Chapter 3
- Part 1. 원인과 결과를 나타내는 구문 & 문장 .... 96 ~ 97
- Part 2. 목적을 나타내는 구 & 문장 .... 98 ~ 99
  - Check Point (12)
- Part 3. 분사 구문 .... 100 ~ 109
  - Exercise (5)
  - Check Point (13)

Chapter 4 접속사
- Part 1. 등위접속사와 병렬구조 .... 112 ~ 113
- Part 2. 상관접속사 .... 114 ~ 116
  - Check Point (14)
- Part 3. 시간, 조건의 부사절 117
- Part 4. 비록 ~일지라도 (양보 절) 그리고 구 118
- Part 5. 복합 관계부사 119
- Part 6. 접속사 as 120
- Part 7. 내가 모를 수도 있는 접속사 .... 121 ~ 123
  - Check Point (15)

Chapter 5 명사절

- Part 1. 명사절 ..... 126 ~ 127
- Part 2. if, whether 128
- Part 3. 명사 역할 의문사 129
- Part 4. what (것) ..... 130 ~ 131
- Part 5. 복합관계 대명사 ..... 132 ~ 134
    - Check Point (16)
    - Stop (5) 배웠는데 자꾸 잊어버리는 구절

Chapter 6 관계대명사

- Part 1. 관계대명사 (주격, 목적격) ..... 136 ~ 139
    - Exercise (6, 7)
- Part 2. 관계사 생략 140
- Part 3. 전치사 + 관계사 141
- Part 4. 소유격 whose 142
- Part 5. 계속적 ..... 143 ~ 144
- Part 6. 수를 나타내는 of 관계대명사 145
- Part 7. 관계사에 삽입 절이 들어 있는 경우 145
- Part 8. 관계부사 ..... 146 ~ 150
    - Exercise (8)
    - Check Point (17 ~ 18)

Chapter 7

- Part 1. 비교급 152
- Part 2. 비교급인데 좀 다르네 153
- Part 3. 원급 비교 154
- Part 4. 최상급 155
- Part 5. 비교급으로 최상급을 표현 ..... 156 ~ 157
    - Check Point (19)

Chapter 8

- Part 1. 도치 ..... 160 ~ 161
- Part 2. 강조 162
- Part 3. 생략 163
- Part 4. 수의 일치 ..... 164 ~ 165
    - Check Point (20)

딱!
한권으로 정리되는
구문독해

Chapter 1

Part 1. **형식에 관한 문장**

Part 2. **나는 주어다!!!**

Part 3. **보어는 주어 혹은 목적어를 보충 설명**

Part 4. **목적어가 필요해!**

Part 1 형식에 관한 문장

1형식: 주어+동사만으로도 의미가 전달이 되는 문장

A bird **flew** to the north.
My baby **cries** every night.

2형식: 주어의 상태나 신분을 나타내는 문장

This boy **is** not **my son**.
She **got upset**.

3형식: 목적어가 필요 해

I want **some water**.
He met **his uncle**.

4형식: 준다고 줘!

I gave **her** some money.
She bought **me** the guitar.

5형식: 목적어의 상태나 신분을 나타내는 문장

I found her **unhappy**.
He made me **a coach**.

1-1 1형식

* 1형식은 목적어 없이 **주어+동사만으로도 문장의 의미가 전달이 되는 문장**을 가리키며 주로 문장 뒤에 동사를 꾸며주는 부사나 시간, 장소를 나타내는 단어가 나온다.

대표동사 (come, go, sleep, fly, happen, work, rise, last, occur...)

> **01** Violent crimes **rise** more in cities than in countries. (자동사: 동사만으로 의미 전달)
> 폭력적인 범죄는 발생한다 더 많이 도시에서 시골에서 보다
>
> **02** The difficulty **lies** in providing sufficient evidence.
> 어려움은 놓여있다 제공하는데 있어 충분한 증거를

03 Patience **pays off**.

04 This medicine **works** well for back pain.

05 Weather **varies** from state to state.

06 It does not **matter** (count) how slowly you go, as long as you do not stop.

07 Will this room **do** or would you prefer one with a shower? (do = enough or acceptable)

08 Your good luck can't **last**. Eventually, things will change.

09 Small earthquakes like these **occur** very often in this region.

10 The rain forest might **disappear** forever if we don't protect it.

11 I **leapt** up the stairs three at a time. (leaped)

12 The custom of arranged marriages still **exists** in many countries.

13 **There are** several people injured in a bomb explosion.

Exercise 1

▶ 다음 중 옳은 것을 고르시오.

01 She (rose / raised) to the top of the mountain at dawn.

02 Bright future (lies / lays) before you, so don't worry.

03 John (rose / raised) his hand because he knew the answer.

04 There is an alarming (rise / raise) in unemployment rate.

05 His complaint (was lasted / lasted) for more than 30 minutes.

▶ 다음 틀린 문장을 고쳐 쓰시오.

01 She lay her baby on the cradle.

02 John rose the curtain to look out the window.

03 The sun is risen from the east.

04 Surprisingly, she raised in a large city.

05 Mike was appeared on a national television.

06 This kind of crime is often happened in a big city.

▶ 다음 주어진 동사를 이용하여 알맞은 형태로 바꾸어 쓰시오.

> rise, raise, lie, lay

01 A full moon _____ over the valley last night.

02 The success of election _____ in people's participation.

03 The cat was _____ dead on the floor.

04 She _____ on the back against the pillow.

05 We are going to _____ fund for the poor.

1-2 2형식

* 주격보어 즉, 동사 다음에 **명사나 형용사**가 나와 **주어의 신분이나 상태**를 나타내는 문장 형식으로 가장 대표적인 동사는 be동사이다.

* 2형식 동사의 종류

    a) 오감 동사 + 형용사가 나와 **주어의 상태**를 나타냄: look (seem, appear), taste, smell, sound, feel

    b) **stay, keep, remain** + 형용사가 나와 **주어의 상태 지속**을 나타낸다. (~상태로) 있다.

    c) **go, get, grow, fall, run, turn, come** + 형용사가 나와 **주어의 상태 변화**를 나타낸다. (~되다)

---

01 **Today is the first day** of the rest of your life.
   오늘은   첫날이다.   너의 삶의 나머지의

02 She **looks** rather **ordinary** today.
   그녀는 보인다   오히려 평범하게   오늘

03 Mike **kept silent** when he was asked about his private life.
   Mike는 침묵을 지켰다   그가 질문을 받았을 때   그의 사생활에 관해

---

04 Her dream **came true**.

05 Good medicine **tastes** bitter.

06 Their complaints **sound** reasonable to me.

07 She **appeared** uninterested in my detailed explanation.

08 She **seems** indifferent to my plan.

09 It is hard to **stay** awake in the middle of the night.

10 For years, the rules of good studying habits have **remained consistent**.

11 Paul managed to **keep alive** by climbing up a tree.

12 The water in the lake will **run dry** soon due to a severe drought these days.

13 He **grew impatient** when no one told him how long he had to wait.

14 He **got nervous** when the detective asked him several questions about the incident.

15 The police are worried that the situation could **turn violent**.

16 Alex **fell silent** and turned his attention to his food.

17 The crowd watching the fight was **going wild** with excitement.

18 Alexia **felt guilty** for not immediately writing her back.

19 A wire had **come loose** at the back.

20 My arm was **becoming** more and more **painful**.

[Part 3: page 38 보어 편에 다시 나올 때 확인 학습함]

Exercise 2

▶ 다음 중 옳은 것을 고르시오.

01 Peter looked as (bright / brightly) as his brother.

02 Stay inside. It's raining (heavy / heavily).

03 He told us a new plan and sounded (fair / fairly).

04 She grew (impatient / impatiently) when he heard the news.

05 The meat has gone (bad / badly).

06 He appears (normal / normally), but he behaves (strange / strangely).

07 He kept (quiet / quietly) all this morning.

▶ 다음 빈칸에 들어 갈 수 없는 것을 고르시오.

01 He and his brother seem _____.

① friendly   ② lovely   ③ lonely   ④ happily   ⑤ big

02 He tried to be as _____ as possible.

① fair   ② calm   ③ simply   ④ quick   ⑤ rich

03 She got _____.

① mad   ② upset   ③ friendly   ④ peaceful   ⑤ busily

04 She talked to me _____.

① friendly   ② happily   ③ directly   ④ kindly   ⑤ nicely

05 My sister sings a song _____.

① lovely   ② pleasantly   ③ elegantly   ④ merrily   ⑤ beautifully

1-3 3형식

* 3형식은 **동사(타동사)** 다음에 바로 목적어를 필요로 하는 문장 형태를 가리키며 목적어 자리에는 명사, 동명사, to-부정사, 구나 혹은 절(주어+동사)가 올 수 있다.

01 I **discussed** the matter with him.
　　나는 토론했다　그 문제를　그와 함께

02 She **will reach** the destination today.
　　그녀는 도달할 것이다.　목적지에　오늘

03 Flies **lay** eggs on decaying meat.

04 I **appreciate** what you have done for me.

05 All the major airlines **have raised** their fares.

06 They are **raising** funds to help needy youngsters.

07 He **laid** his hand on my shoulder.

08 I'm sure she will **survive** this crisis.

09 Large classes **present** great problems **to** many teachers.

10 Her mother often **compares** me **with** her son.

11 He **shares** his room **with** his nephew.

12 Can you **replace** the dead batteries **with** new ones?

13 They will provide us **with** some information on that.

14 His back injury may prevent him **from** playing soccer any more.

15 I can't distinguish him **from** his twin brother.

16 This place always reminds me **of** my first date with my wife.

17 His father left huge inheritance **to** him.

18 I have already delivered the furniture **to** my customer.

19 Can you describe **to me** the man you saw at the crime scene?

20 He blamed me **for** poor safety standards.

21 The police arrested him **for** violating human rights.

22 We try hard to keep people **from** getting our valuable information.

23 His poor eyesight prohibited him **from** becoming a pilot.

24 Sometimes, you must **inform** those close to you **of** upcoming change by conveying important information well in advance.

25 Asians show great care for each other, since they **view** harmony **as** essential to relationship improvement.

1-4 4형식

* 4형식은 동사의 영향을 받는 사람이나 물건이 먼저 나오며 흔히 수여동사라 불리고,
동작을 받는 명사를 ~에게 ~을(해) 주다로 해석한다.

> **01** My mother **gave** me more than she could afford.
>   주었다 나에게   그녀가 줄 수 있는 것 이상으로
>
> **02** I **sent** her a letter of apology with a bunch of flowers.
>   보내주었다 그녀에게   사과의 편지를   꽃 한 다발과 함께

03 While you're out, could you **get me** some batteries?

04 The archeologist **showed** me a few remains of ancient civilization.

05 The club **charged** them an annual membership fee.

06 The accident **cost** the driver of the car the use of his legs.

07 I **owe** my parents a lot for everything they've done for me.

08 Our summer programs **offer** children the opportunity to try a variety of sports activities.

09 My boss allowed me another chance for a promotion.

10 In his will, he will leave all his children a small sum of money.

11 You have to pay them a fee in advance to enter.

12 If these don't work, I may have to prescribe you something stronger.

Exercise 3

▶ 다음 어법상 틀린 부분을 수정하시오.

01 She introduced me her brother yesterday.

02 Can you explain her the accident?

03 Would you please deliver him this furniture?

04 She will show for us how capable she is.

05 Mike informed very important information to us.

06 I would like to discuss about our trip with you.

07 Mike wants to marry with her this year.

08 We will attend to this meeting tomorrow.

09 They can discuss about this matter this afternoon.

▶ 다음 문장을 해석하시오.

01 The bear's sense of smell tells it where prey is hiding.

02 She will ask him whether he is financially independent.

03 It won't cost you a penny for the first six months after you move in.

04 The carpenter built the homeless a shelter to spend the cold winter.

05 Her father will leave her nothing if she doesn't do what she has to do.

06 I can show you how precious this jewel is.

1-5 5형식

*목적어에 대한 보충어인 **명사**, **형용사**가 목적어 다음에 나와 목적어의 **상태**나 **신분**을 나타내며 형용사로 쓰이는 과거분사, 현재분사도 있다. [part 3 보어에서 다시 자세하게 나옴]

01 She considers **the rule = strict**.
　　　　　　　　규칙이　　엄격하다고 (엄격한 규칙)

02 We found **him = an excellent teacher**.
　　　　　　그를　　　훌륭한 교사라고

03 The storm left many people **homeless**.

04 The jury finally found him **guilty** as (he was) charged.

05 He was struggling to prove his son **innocent**.

06 The government will set those prisoners **free** next month.

07 You will find someone I often talk with on the phone **very humble**.

08 He always tries to keep his room **neat and tidy**.

09 There are many ways to make **waking up** more pleasant.

10 Doctors call them placebo effects while psychologists call them non-specific effects.

11 Make an elegantly styled silk blouse a special treat.

12 As she speaks Spanish fluently, it makes her more fascinating.

13 Experts consider the seventeenth century the beginning of modern English.

▶ 다음 중 알맞은 것을 고르시오.

01 We made her (happy / happily).

02 They will keep this puppy (safe / safely).

03 I found driving in a rainy day (dangerous / dangerously).

04 She wants to make her birthday party (great / greatly).

05 I found the test (easy / easily). I got a perfect score.

06 This simple action can make you really (famous / famously).

07 The bright colors will put viewers (comfortable / comfortably).

08 This blanket will make you (warm / warmly).

09 My wife sometimes drives me (crazy / crazily).

10 Please leave every bottle you used (clean / cleanly).

11 You have to look at this problem (different / differently).

12 The rules she set were considered (strict / strictly).

13 You will soon find his house (easy / easily).

14 The noise they made during the meeting drove him (mad / madly).

15 We need to find some toys to keep the kids (amusing / amused).

Part 2 나는 주어다 !!!

*주어는 명사만 될 수 있지만 명사 역할을 하는 to-부정사, 동명사, 구, 절(주어+동사)도 주어가 될 수 있고 몇 가지 예외적인 경우를 제외하고는 문장 맨 앞에 나옵니다. 주어는 항상 (은, 는, 이, 가) 조사가 붙어야 해석이 무난하게 됩니다.

2-1. 주어 위치에 명사구가

To work with her is fun. (to-부정사 주어)

Hiring a new employee is my job. (동명사 주어)

2-2. 주어 위치에 절이

That she was a spy was true.

What she gave me was a watch.

2-3. 가주어 It ~ to

It is easy to make a cake.

It is fun for me to spend time with her.

2-4. 가주어 It ~ that

It is true that she works at a bank.

It is up to her whether he will come here or not.

2-5. 그냥 가져다 쓸게요. 관용적인 용법의 주어 It

It seems that she works for Jenny.

It is likely that she will marry John soon.

2-6. It is ~ that 강조

It is Jenny that John loves.

It was last week that Mike left for London.

2-7. 주어를 뒤에서 꾸미는 말이 형용사, to 부정사, 분사

The food to prepare for them is vegetables

The man working for me is older than me.

2-8. 주어를 꾸며주는 말이 길다: 관계사

The child who I am taking care of is my niece.

The machine he uses at the shop often breaks down.

2-9. 주어를 꾸며주는 관계부사

The reason why she was fired was that she neglected her duty.

2-10. 동격의 that

The fact that she moved to London was shocking.

2-11. 주어를 꾸며주는 전치사구

The lady in the waiting room is not my mom.

2-1 명사구 주어 (구: 2개 이상의 단어가 일정한 순서대로 모여 하나의 역할을 함)

* **to-부정사나 혹은 동명사가 주어로 사용되는 경우** 뒤에 꾸며주는 말이 같이 나와서 주어가 상당히 길게 전개 될 수도 있다.

> **01** **To argue with him about political issues** is a waste time.
> 정치적 화제에 대해서 그와 논쟁하는 것은   시간낭비이다.
>
> **02** **Improving one's language ability** is important in a society.
> 한 사람의 언어능력을 향상시키는 것은   중요하다   사회에서

03 To adapt yourself to the new environment **takes** some time.

04 To work with other people in harmony **becomes** a major factor for success.

05 To keep a note of your passport number **is** sensible.

06 Treating other people without prejudice is important.

07 Being the President of a nation is in the hand of God.

08 Paying attention to the class is another good habit in studying.

09 Organizing one thing at a time is a way of saving time.

10 Forming the basis of marriage is trust and love.

11 Having diverse cultures makes our country special and imaginative.

12 Keeping indoor temperatures moderate at all times for the patients is important.

13 Avoiding the issue often uses up a great deal of energy without resolving the worsening situation.

2-2 주어 위치에 절(주어+동사): 명사절, 관계대명사, 관계부사...

* 명사절을 이끄는 접속사 that, whether, 관계사 what, 관계부사, 복합관계사 whatever는 주어로 사용될 수 있다. 명사구와 마찬가지로 주어 문장이 긴 경우 동사를 확인해야한다.

01 **That she will marry soon** is a rumor. (주로 가주어로 전환해서 사용)
그녀가 곧 결혼한다는 것은 소문이다. (It is a rumor that she will marry soon)

02 **Whether I should stay here or not** is uncertain.
내가 여기에 머물러야 하는지 아닌지는 확실하지 않다.

03 **What makes me uncomfortable** is her attitude.
나를 불편하게 하는 [것은] 그녀의 태도이다.

04 **Whatever you experience** will help   you improve   your performance.
당신이 경험하는 것이 [무엇이던지] 도와줄 것입니다 당신이 향상시키도록 당신의 수행을

05 **Whoever wants to see me** has to make an appointment first.
나를 보고 싶은 사람은 [누구이던지] 먼저 약속을 잡아야 합니다.

06 **Where most celebrities reside** is unknown to the public.
대부분의 유명인사가 거주하는 [곳은] 대중들에게 알려져 있지 않다.

07 **How he treats his employees** is polite.

08 **What those children need** is some love and affection.

09 **Why she refused his offer** was that the pay was too low.

10 **What this indicates** is that over 81% of teachers are dissatisfied with their pay.

11 **Whether she can have access to the information or not** depends on her capability.

12 **The way the police set a strategy for dealing with crime** was very fast and brief.

2-3 가주어 It ~ to

* 주어가 to-부정사인 경우 대부분 가주어의 형식으로 사용하며, 문장에서 실질적인 주어는 아니지만 **for (of)** 다음에 나오는 **목적어**가 주어처럼 해석이 되어 의미상의 주어라 불린다.

> **01** It is impossible **to cancel** our trip to Europe now.
>   불가능하다   취소하는 것은   우리의 여행을 유럽으로 지금
>
> **02** It is important **to bring** an imaginative solution to the waste problem.
>   중요하다   가져오는 것은   상상력이 풍부한 해결방법을   쓰레기 문제에 대해

03 It is my duty **to find out** how destructive the modern weapons are.

04 It is difficult **to know** how to determine whether one culture is better than another.

05 It is generous **of him** to offer me a plane fare.

06 It is necessary **for a speaker** to memorize his or her script to reduce on-stage anxiety.

07 It is imperative for every employee to meet face-to-face with the client.

08 It is natural for her to get mad at John when he teases her.

09 It is never too late to learn anything. (날씨, 날짜, 요일, **시간**, 거리, 명암의 비 인칭 It)

10 It is worth seeing that movie more than twice. (동명사 가주어)

11 It is no use denying the fact. (동명사 가주어)

12 This material is too complicated **for us** to use. (의미상의 주어)

13 Adequate expectations leave room **for many experiences** to be pleasant surprises. (의미상의 주어)

2-4 나도 가주어 It ~ that 혹은 It ~ whether

*That 혹은 Whether로 시작하는 경우에 주로 가주어를 사용한다.

01 **That her brother enabled her to study abroad** is true.
= It is true **that her brother enabled her to study abroad**.
진실이다　　그녀의 brother가 가능하게 했다는 것이 그녀가 해외에서 공부하는 것을

02 It **is our company's policy** that **all new employees must go through** the training programs.
　　우리 회사의 정책이다　　　　　　모든 새 직원들이 거쳐야 하는 것은 (주어)　　　　훈련 과정을

03 It **is no wonder** that the force of gravity has a great effect on us.
　　당연 합니다　　　　중력의 힘이 우리에게 큰 영향을 미치는 것은

04 It **is said** that he used to be a famous singer in Korea. (~라고 한다)
　　　　　그는 한국에서 유명한 가수였다라고 한다.

05 It is a fact **that** many deaths from lung cancer are caused by smoking.

06 It is obvious **that** we can't get access to the building without the permission of the owner.

07 It is often mentioned **that** only those who dare to fail greatly can ever achieve greatly.

08 While it may be true that vitamin C does prevent colds, no one can claim that.

09 It is thought that scientists are making effort to make widespread use of the technology.

10 It is expected that people may become impatient with one another if they see each other frequently.

11 It is certain that the value of the dollar on international markets has declined significantly over the past year.

12 It depends on you **whether** she will financially support our organization.

2-5 그냥 가져다 쓸게요! 흔히 관용적인 용법이라 함

*가주어처럼 해석되지 않으며, 단지 필요에 의해 It을 주어로 사용하는 경우: seem, be likely

01 It **seems to be a current trend** not to wear suits and ties at work.
　　　　　현재 경향인 것처럼 보인다

02 It **seems** that these works **will turn out** to be genuine. (that절의 동사와 seem을 붙여서 해석)
　　　이 작품들은 진짜인 것으로 판명될 것처럼 보인다.

03 It **is likely** that he **will be fired** from his job soon. (동사와 같이 붙여서 해석)
　　　그는 해고될 것 같다.　　　　그의 직업에서 곧 (해고 될 것이다 + ~일 것 같다)

04 It seems that what she did was right.

05 It doesn't seem that we are welcome here.

06 It didn't seem that he appreciated what I had done for him.

07 It appears that human beings are the only creatures capable of abstract thought.

08 It is likely that the meeting will be postponed this week.

09 It is likely that staring computer screens too long will damage our eyes.

10 It seems unlikely that unemployment rate will fall below 3% this year. (~일 것처럼 보이지 않는다)

11 If you've upset somebody, chances are that they'll carry their anger with them.

12 It is most likely that Black people receive Covid fines in England and Wales.

13 If you are having problems with your asthma, it most likely means that you are not on an appropriate treatment plan.

2-6 It is ~ that 강조문장

* 'It + be동사 + 강조할 말 + that + 나머지 부분'의 문장 구조 형태
  강조할 말에는 '사람, 사물, 시간 부사구, 장소 부사구'가 들어갈 수 있다. 동사는 강조 불가능

> **01** He himself ruined his own reputation.
> = It was **his own reputation** that he himself ruined.
>   바로 그의 명성이였다 　　　　　그 스스로가 망친 것은
>
> **02** It was **in China** that the Corona virus first broke out.
>   바로 중국에서였다 　　　코로나 바이러스가 처음 발생한 것은

03 What do you want? = What **is it that** you want?

04 **It was** in New Zealand **that** Elizabeth first met Mr. Williams.

05 **It is** you **who** are to blame.

06 It was Mike who didn't accomplish his own task.

07 It is the atmosphere that she likes about the restaurant.

08 It was about the definition of life that they had different opinions.

09 It was in New York City that most of the first immigrants to the U. S settled down.

10 It is in south Texas that the destruction of the bird's habitats has been most alarming.

11 It was at her laboratory that they conducted many types of experiments on rats.

12 It was then that I realized rejection is easier to accept when you're honest with yourself about the reasons why.

13 It was the moment that she, Washington, John, and everyone else who built the bridge had worked so hard for. (교과서 참조)

❖ 해석이 안 된다고 뒤로 가면 더 혼란!!

01 To see the faults of others is easy, but to find those of your own is quite hard.

02 It is a sad phenomenon that most people pay little attention to their health.

03 It is silly of her to believe what he said.

04 It is safe that children take antibiotics in liquid form.

05 It seems likely that they will soon release the hostages.

06 What may be a normal behavior in one culture may seem inappropriate or even rude in another.

07 It is said that his identical twin brother can be distinguished by the way he dresses.

08 It is often said that solar energy is the best alternative energy for the future.

09 It was at this palace that our troop surrendered to the enemy.

10 Thinking it is inevitable that doctors will make the occasional mistake / is wrong.

11 It is necessary to cultivate our realistic optimism by combining a positive attitude with an honest assessment of the challenges. (combine A with B: A와 B를 결합시키다)

12 Neglecting to consume sufficient amounts of fruits and vegetables can result in an increased risk of cancer.

13 Asking students to evaluate teachers is a recommendable policy that will enhance the quality of teachers.

2-7 주어 뒤에 꾸미는 말이 형용사, to 부정사, 분사

＊주어 다음에 꾸며주는 수식어가 형용사나, 부정사, 현재, 과거분사가 나오는 경우
 동사의 위치를 먼저 찾는 것이 해석하기에 용이하다.

01 [The bag] **full of cash** suddenly disappeared. (앞 명사를 꾸며주는 형용사구)
 현금으로 가득 찬 가방이   갑자기   사라졌다.

02 [Money] **to buy some food** is not good enough. (앞 명사를 꾸며주는 to-부정사구)
 음식을 살 돈이   충분하지가 않다.

03 [Time] **devoted to teaching children** is very precious. (앞에 명사를 꾸며주는 과거분사)
 아이들을 가르치는데 헌신된 시간은   매우 귀중하다.

04 [The lady] **waiting for her turn** looked furious. (앞에 명사를 꾸며주는 현재분사)
 그녀의 순서를 기다리는 여성이   격분한 것처럼 보였다.

05 A chance **to beat** him in the race is slim.

06 People **living** in an urban area work fewer hours.

07 The global efforts **to deal** with air pollution won't bring any results.

08 The man **found** in the cave used to be a soldier.

09 Freud's attempts **to interpret** the meaning of dreams became successful.

10 Clothing **appropriate** for the temperature and environmental conditions is good for exercise.

11 His financial problem **to overcome** seems far away.

12 Illiterate people **educated** by the aid of the government now enjoy reading news articles.

13 Watching the boy **carried** away in an ambulance made me sad.

14 Crimes committed these days are getting more and more violent.

15 The watches imported from Switzerland are popular among the young.

16 Death and destruction brought about by the floods left people desperate.

17 A 10-year-old first learning to swim waits to overcome the hesitation before jumping.

18 Greenpeace interested in protecting the environment is an international organization.

19 The issues referred to during the meeting yesterday are likely to be resolved sooner or later.

20 People often violating traffic laws never think about the possibility of getting into accidents.

21 Expenses related to the company's trading activities shouldn't be excessive.

22 Keeping good ideas floating around in your head is a great way to ensure that they won't happen.

23 We can do two things at the same time if the tasks or activities involved require quite different kinds of attention.

24 The persons put in the situation of buying a calculator that cost $15 found out from the vendor that the same product was available in a different store 20 minutes away and at a promotional price of $10.

2-8 주어를 꾸며 주는 관계대명사 주격, 목적격, 소유격, what

*관계대명사를 형용사 절이라 하며 앞에 나온 명사를 꾸며주는 역할을 한다. [page 135]

01 The micro dust ⇐ **that blows into Korea from China** / has been a serious problem.
중국으로부터 한국으로 불어오는 미세먼지는   심각한 문제가 되어왔다

관계사 who 앞에 those는 일반사람들을 가리킴
02 [Those] **who have an intention of doing something good** / might not be unhappy though they fail.
좋은 일을 하는 것의 의도를 가진 사람들은 (좋은 의도를 가지고 알을 하는 사람들은)

03 [All] **we know about her** is her name. (All이 선행사인 문장의 동사는 항상 is)
우리가 그녀에 대해 알고 있는 것은 단지 그녀의 이름이다.

04 [The girl] **whose father is a policeman** feels proud of him. (whose: 가진, ~의) [page 142]
경찰관인 아버지가 있는 소녀는   그를 자랑스럽게 여긴다.

05 [What] **has value for one** may be worthless to another. [page 130]
한 사람에게 가치 있는 [것은]   가치가 없을지도 모른다 다른 사람에게

06 The wealth **which we all want to enjoy** is not easy to obtain.

07 Miners **who are exposed to uranium dust** are more likely to get lung cancer.

08 A lot of our medicines **that are used to treat patients** originate from tropical plants.

09 The man who earns a huge income rather leads a moderate life.

10 The animals that inhabit that area are endangered to be extinct.

11 The company that benefits its employees in many ways will expand rapidly.

12 Kids who hardly play develop brains 20% to 50% smaller than normal.

[Chapter 6에서 관계대명사에 대한 전반적인 내용이 나옴.]

13 The number of friends that most people have is limited to only a few.

14 The greatest mistake a man can make is to be afraid of making one.

15 More than 50 percent of the land which she owns is used for agriculture.

16 The physics which I hate to study will be a big barrier against me.

17 The project which our team has developed will generate a lot of jobs.

18 The personal information that we hold is secure and used in a respectful manner.

19 The man whose house burned down will go into the shelter.

20 The girl whose handwriting is the best in my class is Jenny.

21 All they have to do to not get infected is (to) stay home.

22 All you have to learn is that traditions provide us with the values and inner strength.

23 What her attitude indicates is that she has no intention of working here any more.

24 What really matters in a pencil is not its wooden outside, but the carbon inside.

25 Some of the ways people think that they can cure pimples or control them are really just myths.

26 People who experience an incredible success end up longing for that experience long after it has gone.

CHECK POINT 2

❖ **항상 시작이 어렵지만 그렇다고 멈출 수는 없잖아.**

01 From now on, anyone whose ticket has been stamped may enter the auditorium.

02 The course he is willing to take from this week places emphasis on practical work.

03 Those who had more positive expectations for success do better in the following weeks, months, and years.

04 The poison that this fish produces is a lot more poisonous than the chemical which is usually used to kill rats.

05 Much of the great progress the human race has made during the past four centuries has been brought by new inventions.

06 The amount of physical exercise that you perform during the day is one of the key ingredients to helping you get a good night's sleep.

07 The obese women who were confident that they would succeed lost 26 pounds more than self-doubters.

08 Having the ability to take care of oneself without depending on others was considered a requirement for everyone.

09 Individuals who are forced to work in a style that does not fit them may perform below their actual capabilities.

10 The people who are less happy are those with desires that are much higher than what they already have.

2-9 주어를 꾸며주는 관계부사 (where, when, why, how)

*관계부사 - 장소, 시간, 이유, 방법을 나타내며 **전치사 + 관계대명사**를 의미한다.
[관계부사 다음에 나오는 문장이 해석 가능하다: page 146]

01 **[The reason why] she tries to restrict class size** is absolutely clear.
그녀가 수업크기를 제한하려고 노력하는 이유는

02 **[The way] they carved the statue from a single block of marble** surprised us.
그들이 대리석의 하나의 블록으로부터 동상을 새겼던 방법은

03 **The place where this animal inhabits** is protected by the city.

04 **The time when she got first pregnant** was probable 30.

05 **The hotel where** we spent our honeymoon has been demolished.

06 The hall where you're giving your talk has a really good sound system.

07 The week when we booked our holiday was warm and sunny.

08 The reason why they decided to cross the border is that they are suffering from starvation.

09 The way people treat you says more about them than it does about you.

10 How you dress can impact the way people perceive you.

2-10 동격의 that 접속사 (추상 명사 + 생략 불가한 that)

* that 다음에 나오는 내용이 앞에 나온 명사와 같은 것(내용)을 가리킨다.

01 **The feeling = that she might hide something from me** made me confused.
그녀가 나에게 뭔가를 숨길지도 모른다는 느낌은 　　　　　　　　　만들었다 나를 혼란스럽게

02 **The evidence = that she is guilty** has yet not been presented to the court.
그녀가 유죄라는 증거는 　　　　　　아직 제시되지 않았습니다 / 법원에

03 **The belief = that we will find a cure for cancer soon** is obvious.

04 **The assumption** that leaders are born is not accurate.

05 **The mere fact** that Olivia exists somewhere makes me happy.

06 The idea that knowledge is something to be learned will inspire him.

07 The news that she will retire from her position spread like wildfire.

08 The opinion that travelling broadens our horizons is obvious.

09 The hope that their shares will go up in value can come true.

10 Despite the proof that men can raise their children, most women still do not trust them.

11 Our organization was founded on **the belief** that all animals should be respected and treated with kindness, and must be protected by law.

2-11 주어를 꾸며주는 전치사구!!!

*전치사 다음에는 항상 명사나 동명사가 나오므로 먼저 전치사(구)를 해석 한 다음에 해석합니다.

01 [The questions] on this paper are too difficult for 10-year-olds.
　　　이 시험에서 질문들은　　　　　　너무 어렵다　　10세 아이들에게

02 [A meeting] for April 18th will be arranged for them.
　　　4월 18일에 대한 회의는　　　준비될 것이다　그들을 위해

03 [One outcome] of motivation is behavior that takes considerable effort.
　　　동기부여의 한 결과는　　　　　행동이다　　　상당한 노력을 필요로 하는

04 [Reforms] in education are absolutely necessary for our children.
　　　교육에서 개혁은　　　　　우리 아이들에게 절대적으로 필요합니다.

05 **Violence against elderly people** is often reported on TV.

06 **A marriage without love** won't last long.

07 **Growing a high quality product at a reasonable cost** is a key aspect to farming.

08 A tall gentleman with a beard donated a huge amount of money to the charity.

09 The store on the opposite side of the street will go bankrupt.

10 The early death of his business partner due to overwork gave him a new perspective on life.

11 Sometimes it is possible to overlook the fact that the view we take of the objects is important in explaining their form.

❖ 오늘 걷지 않으면 내일은 뛰어야 한다.

01 The laboratory where he conducted the experiment on animals was permanently closed.

02 The reason why most consumers choose this product is that it delivers cost efficiency.

03 The fact that people complain that there is too much violence on TV is often ignored.

04 Cooperation between generations will have a great effect on the society.

05 Peace among the three tribes can bring an enormous amount of energy.

06 The idea that we can live equally and get equal opportunities in this capitalistic society is an illusion.

07 The question of what zebras can gain from having stripes has puzzled scientists for more than a century.

08 Requirements that children should be vaccinated before they attend school play a central role in reducing occurrence of vaccine-preventable diseases.

09 The assumption that birds are descended from dinosaurs has been brought into question by new fossil discoveries in the last few years.

10 The number of people waiting for organ transplants throughout the world is greater than the number of organs available.

11 The judge had taken the view that the fact that medication and regular medication were required was sufficient to show a need for care and attention.

Part 3 보어는 주어 혹은 목적어를 보충 설명

1. 주어를 보충설명 해 주는 명사나 형용사

He is **a soldier**. (그는 군인)
She looks **happy**. (그녀는 행복한)

2. 목적어를 보충설명 해 주는 명사나 형용사

They call **me** = **Jack**. (나를 잭이라고)
I will keep **this room** = **clean**. (이방을 깨끗이)

3. 목적어의 보어가 to-부정사

She wants **me** = **to be quiet**.
　　　　　내가　조용히 하기를

4. 목적어의 보어가 동사원형

He made **her** = **go** home.
　　　　그녀가 가도록

5. 목적어의 보어가 현재분사 (~ing)

She found **a girl** = **waiting** for me.
　　　　소녀를　기다리고 있는

6. 목적어의 보어가 과거분사인 경우

I heard **the bridge** = **finally completed**.
　　　　다리가　　　마침내 완성된

3-1 보어는 주어이다.

*주격 보어는 명사 (to-부정사, 동명사)나 형용사(분사)가 나와 **주어를 보충 설명하는 역할**을하며, 그 이외에도 접속사 that, whether, 관계사 what도 보어 역할을 할 수 있다.

> **01** **His intentions** were **pure and sincere** at first.
> 　　그의 의도들은　　　 =　　　순수하고 진지했다　　처음에는
>
> **02** **The challenge** is **to find** a way to have proper expectations.
> 　　어려움은　　　찾는 것이다 방법을　　　갖는 적절한 기대치를
>
> **03** **The truth** is that no single person has done anything invaluable.
> 　　진실은　　　　한사람 혼자서 하지 않았다는 것이다　　귀중한 일을

04 Stress is **a contributing factor** in many illnesses.

05 She looks **more intelligent** than her sister.

06 We stood **still and watched** as the deer came closer.

07 The first thing to do is **inspiring and motivating** the team.

08 The problem is that the competitive player belongs to another team.

09 This is what we have been looking forward to seeing.

10 What matters most to me is your safety.

11 What made him leave early was his urgent appointment.

12 All he demanded while staying here was a little food. (All = only)

13 All you have to do is keep following your dream.

3-2 목적어 다음에 명사나 형용사가 (5형식)

* 목적어가 바로 보어고, 보어가 목적어!
  목적어 다음에 명사 혹은 형용사가 나와 목적어의 신분이나, 상태를 나타낸다.

> **01** We consider **Mike an excellent teacher**.
>   Mike는 = 훌륭한 선생님
>
> **02** We should keep **the decision making process = simple**.
>   의사 결정과정을 = 단순한
>
> **03** Please leave **the next two lines blank** for the tutor's comments.
>   내버려 두세요   다음 두 줄을   빈칸으로

04 The jury finally found **her not innocent** with the new evidence presented.

05 The Internet has made **so much free information available** on any issue.

06 They will make **using a cell phone while driving illegal**.

07 Try to set your goal realistic or your life will be a disaster.

08 Her mother made John and his brother what they are today.

09 Tears keep the delicate surface of the eyeball clean and wet.

10 The sponsor appointed the only girl among them captain.

11 Many people consider not sending a reply immediately inconsiderate.

12 Mike will keep everything the children use in his classroom clean and safe.

13 Many scientists consider Einstein the greatest physicist of his time.

3-3 목적어 다음에 to-부정사가

*목적어 다음에 to-부정사를 취하는 동사 (want, like, allow, expect, advise...)

01 I encouraged **him to be** a more reliable person.
　　　나는 격려했다　그를　되도록　좀 더 믿음직한 사람이

02 She advised **me to make** a reasonable request.
　　　　　　　　나에게　하라고　　　타당한 요청을

03 I have asked the builders **to give** an estimate for fixing the roof.

04 Your carelessness can cause them **to face** a disaster.

05 She allowed me **to extend** my stay in London for two weeks.

06 Our professor will ask all of us to define the meaning of life in class.

07 We expected the manufacturers to meet the demand for gear against Covid-19.

08 His big success may bring about other people to look smaller in comparison.

09 A researcher wanted the women to tell him what their roads to success would be like.

10 What could possibly lead him to quit working for Jenny?

11 I finally managed to persuade her to extend the deadline.

12 This continuously variable climate forces many natives to change houses twice a year.

13 Acceptance enables you not to have to hide things about yourself and to find freedom to be yourself.

3-4 목적어 다음에 동사원형이!

* 문장에서 동사가 **사역동사나 지각동사**인 경우 목적어 다음에 동사원형이 나온다. (*help는 to-가능)

01 You can **make** [success] **happen** through careful planning and choosing the right strategies.
너는　만들 수 있다　성공이　일어나도록　　신중한 계획과 옳은 전략을 선택하는 것을 통해서
(사역동사) (목적어) (동사원형)

02 I **have seen** [many companies] **rush** their products or services to market too quickly.
나는 보았다　　많은 회사들이　서둘러 내보내는 것을 그들의 제품이나 서비스를 시장에 너무 빨리
(지각동사) (목적어) (동사원형)

03 This man helped us (to) **choose** some tropical fruit and enjoy an exotic atmosphere.

04 Let me look at what factors **affect** the performances of each individual.

05 It is necessary to make a person **feel** a great sense of importance.

06 I will have Jason show you how this machine works.

07 The director watched her imitate your action and the way you speak.

08 He saw a man get out of the vehicle and walk to the side of the road.

09 I heard the voice of the devil say to me I should stop studying and hang out with my friends.

10 We felt the ground shake and dashed to the door.

11 They will make the boy who broke the window pay for the damage.

12 Her attitude toward her body and not to let others tell her how she should look left a deep impression to millions of women.

3-5 목적어 다음에 현재 분사가 (현재분사는 형용사)

*주어가 목적어가 어떤 행위를 하는 과정을 목격한 경우 혹은 진행 중인 경우를 표현하는 경우

01 I found **my whole body [loosening up and at ease]** after the test.
　　 나는 알았다　　나의 전신이　　느슨해지고　　편안한 (나는 느슨해지고 편안해지는 나의 전신을)

02 She noticed **one of her pupils [approaching]** for advice.
　　 그녀는 알아챘다　그녀의 학생들 중의 한 명이　다가오는　　조언을 위해

03 I heard him **[criticizing** and **complaining]** about the government policy on education.
　　 나는 들었다　그가 비판하고　　불평하는 것을　　정부 정책에 대해　　교육에 관한

04 He noticed a woman in a black dress **sitting** across from him.

05 Mike kept the engine **running** to find what's wrong with it.

06 Her remarks left us **wondering** who she wanted to support.

07 I overheard them having a debate about managerial position.

08 When I caught him staring at me, he seemed embarrassed.

09 We watched moon hiding the sun from my hotel room.

10 I saw many refugees begging for a place to stay.

11 We employers sometimes observe employees turning to one another for help.

12 He noticed a woman in a black dress sitting across from him.

13 Very young children who watch television programs featuring violent scenes display (v) more violent behavior within their home environment than do the children who do not.

3-6 목적어 다음에 과거분사가 (목적어에 동작이 가해지는 경우)

*목적어에게 동작이 가해지는 경우를 나타냄: 목적격 수동태, 지각 동사

01 I had my picture **[taken]**.
　　나는　　나의 사진을 찍었다

02 I have seen many houses **[flooded]** in the recent storm.
　　　보았다　　　많은 집들을　⇐　범람되는　　　최근 폭풍으로

03 How would like to get your hair **[done]**?
　　당신의 머리가 어떻게 되었으면 하나요?

04 If you want something to be done, you need to have your voice **heard**.

05 She found the letter from John **torn** in pieces.

06 From now on, whatever happens here has to keep me **informed**. (posted)

07 The terrible accident left him paralyzed for good.

08 Many of the tourists got their wallets stolen at the festival.

09 In order to have your song known to people, it has to be televised.

10 Your competitor saw your new product advertised on TV last night.

11 Why don't you have your children exposed to classical music more frequently?

12 The criminal had his mug shot taken and then got imprisoned.

❖ 목표는 명확한 해석을 통한 이해력

01 She felt hot tears running down her face.

02 They encouraged us to pursue our dream.

03 He had us realize that dealing with people is the most important aspect of our work.

04 You should have your car battery recharged before departure.

05 The difference is that motorists have a choice of whether or not to wear a helmet.

06 What we want you to do is have an optimistic perspective on the future of humanity.

07 The only thing that they fear is that they don't have immunity to the disease.

08 All I am asking you is do the job right and keep everything in place.

09 Globalization has apparently made western culture more familiar to people in developing countries.

10 I detected a strange scratching noise coming from the kitchen.

11 One of the keys to reducing poverty in developing nations is improving educational opportunities for children.

12 A major disadvantage of genetically modified crops is that the plants lack genetic diversity, so they are more exposed to some diseases.

13 The owners of one giant chain store decided to refuse anyone caught for stealing goods shopping in their stores for the rest of his life.

❖ 모르면 해석이 안 되는 필수 구문

* by ~ing: ~함으로써 / in ~ing: 하는데 있어, ~할 때 / on ~ing: ~하자마자

01 I appreciate all the effort you've put **in teaching** and wish you a happy retirement.
　　나는 감사하다　모든 노력을　네가 쏟은　　가르치는데 있어

02 You should market yourself to the persons **by sending** a good message to them.
　　당신은 당신자신을 홍보해야한다　　사람들에게　　보냄으로써

03 **On finding** his intention to resign, his rival was relieved.
　　사임하려는 그의 의도를 알자마자,　　　그의 경쟁자는 안도했다.

04 **In trying to protect** endangered animals, she asked for government aid.

05 You will be confronted with a lot of problems **in managing** that organization.

06 A yearly income of $24,000 will not help me **in meeting** my financial obligations right away.

07 People should keep their refrigerator from working too hard **by letting** hot foods cool.

08 Everyone can play a part in reducing packaging waste **by changing** their buying habits.

09 Positive expectations are more effective than fantasizing about a desired future, and they are likely to increase your chances of success **in achieving** goals.

10 **By knowing** the speed of sound and measuring the time it takes to hear echo, you can calculate the distance of the object.

11 Since the way we learn is **by making** mistakes, the greatest risk of all is to wait too long to begin making those mistakes.

Part 4 목적어가 필요해

1. 명사를 목적어로 취하는 동사

I met **a beautiful wife**.
을, 를

2. to-부정사 목적어

She wants **to meet** me.
만나기를

3. 동명사가 목적어

He finished **cleaning up** the house.
청소하는 것을

4. 명사절(주어+동사) 목적어

I believe **that she works too hard**.
그녀가 열심히 일하는 것을 (일한다고)

5. 가목적어

She made **it** possible for me **to use** my computer
사용하는 것을

6. 전치사 목적어

She is looking **at the tower**.
탑을

7. 재귀 목적어

We all love **ourselves**.
우리 자신들을

4-1 목적어 자리에 명사는 기본!!!

*주어 + 동사 + 명사 (목적어)

01 These changes will involve **everyone** in the group.
　　 이 변화들은 포함할 것이다.　　　 모두를　　　모임 안에

02 After two hours, we finally reached **the coast**.
　　 두시간 후에　　 우리는 마침내 도달했다　　 해안에

03 I requested **permission** to leave early for my personal business.
　　 나는 요청했다　 허락을　　　떠날　 일찍　　나의 개인적인 일을 위해

04 Campbell's broken leg will probably require **surgery**.

05 Hungary established **diplomatic relations** with Chile in 1990.

06 The mechanic estimated **the cost of repairs** at $350.

07 Analysts are discussing possible causes of the air crash.

08 The helmet law should reduce injuries in motorcycle accidents.

09 The government should restore public confidence in the education system.

10 We must try to distribute the country's wealth so that we help those who need it most.

11 Her experience as a refugee informs the content of her latest novel.

12 They have approved the use of a new drug for lung cancer.

4-2 목적어가 to-부정사

* **의미가 바뀌는 동사**: manage to: 간신히 ~ 하다 / happen to: 우연히 ~ 하다
  mean to: ~할 작정이다 / stop to: ~ 하기 위하여 / stop ~ing: 하는 것을 멈추다
  remember (forget) to: ~할 것을 기억하다 / remember (forget) ~ing: ~했던 것을 기억하다

---

01 This boy **tends to have** relatively better visual abilities.
　　이 소년은　　갖는 경향이 있다　　상대적으로 더 좋은 시각적 능력을

02 He **hesitated to contact** her elder sister after an argument.
　　　연락하는 것을 망설였다　　그의 누나에게　　논쟁 후에

03 She **happened to be involved** in an argument with a stranger.
　　　우연히 관여하게 되었다　　어떤 논쟁에　　낯선 사람과

---

04 He is willing **to stay** here another month if she approves of his request.

05 The detective is still trying **to determine** the cause of the murder.

06 I could manage **to get along** quite well with other colleagues.

07 She is likely to ruin his chances of winning the election.

08 The employees came to know the significant change in their work environment.

09 She pretended not to understand what he was trying to say.

10 Mike prefers to come here with you rather than stay there.

11 Joe refused to accept his offer due to the distance to work.

12 You can't afford to miss this kind of opportunity.

13 Please don't stop to take any valuables when there is a fire.

4-3 목적어가 동명사 (finish, enjoy, mind, give up, avoid, deny,..)

01 My mom **finished decorating** the house with new ornaments.
나의 엄마는　　장식하는 것을 마쳤다　　　집을 새로운 장식품으로

02 He **avoids talking** with his girlfriend about their marriage.
그는 대화하는 것을 피한다.　그의 여자친구와　　그들의 결혼에 대해

03 Tourism will **stop generating** more income for local communities.
관광은　　창출하는 것을 멈출 것이다　　더 많은 소득을　지역사회를 위해

04 She suggested **delaying** the trip to Europe until next year.

05 Mike remembers **encountering** stress and difficulties which he had to overcome. (*)

06 The company gave up **manufacturing** the bike due to the high cost of production.

07 Big companies often delay paying their bills to their contractors.

08 She denied saying that she had witnessed the man at the crime scene.

09 I can't help thinking about you all the time. = I can't help but think about you all the time.

10 The man in black admitted causing death by reckless driving.

11 She **got fed up with** having to examine all the details. [질리다]

12 She could **get used to** controlling her anger by taking a deep breath.

13 We **are accustomed to** using audio to present examples of language in use.

4-4 목적어가 주어+동사 (명사 자리에 접속사 that, whether + 주어 + 동사)

*that 다음에 나오는 동사를 ~라고, 혹은 ~인 것을 이라고 해석하면 적절 [page 126]

01 I think　**that the majority of residents here are decent citizens.**
　　　나는 생각한다　　　여기 거주자들의 대다수가　　　　좋은 시민들이라고

02 He argues　**that being virtuous means finding a balance.**
　　　그는 주장한다　　미덕 있는 것이　　의미한다고　　균형을 찾는 것을

03 Your attitude indicates **whether you are living life or life is living you.**
　　　너의 태도는 가리킨다.　　　　네가 삶을 살고 있는지　　　삶이 너를 살고 있는지를

04 We are all aware **that we live in an era of instant communication.**

05 Biologists believe **that a small amount of radiation exposure** is of greater benefit than harm.

06 She says **that we need a considerable amount of time to restore the economy**.

07 I don't understand that you persist in blaming yourself for what happened.

08 He insists that children should learn work ethics early as possible.

09 Analysis of texts has shown that men and women tend to have different styles of writing.

10 The growing consumer debt indicates that more and more people may be letting their spending habits get out of hand.

11 We wonder whether or not the government has any kind of policy that can protect the victims from criminals.

4-5 목적어가 가짜래!

* 목적어로 사용된 to-부정사나 혹은 that 절이 너무 긴 경우에 그 자리에 의미 없는 it을 쓰고 **to-부정사 또는 that** 문장을 뒤로 보내는 형태의 문장이다.

01 I think **it** awkward **to talk** with someone I meet for the first time.
나는 생각한다 어색하다고 대화하는 것을   내가 처음 만난 사람과

02 You will find **it** difficult **to satisfy** all the customers you deal with.
너는 알 것이다 어렵다고 만족시키는 것을 모든 고객을 네가 다루는

03 He tried to make **it** appear **that** he had done everything himself.
그는 만들려고 노력했다 보이도록   그가 모든 것을 혼자서 해냈다고

04 She considers it effective **to gather** opinions from each member of the club.

05 Their conflict made it worse **to restore** peace in that region.

06 I found it efficient **to rent** a car instead of buying one.

07 They think it sorrowful to leave my family behind to make a living.

08 I believe it nice to treat people equally regardless of race.

09 He made it a rule never to make any friend who could not be useful to him.

10 We believe it the general principle **that education should be available to all children**.

11 We just took it for granted that the $5000 was part of the normal fee for buying a house.

4-6 목적어로 전치사구가 등장!!! (덩어리로 나오는 전치사)

01 The company is proud **of** its achievement.
     회사는   자랑스럽다   회사의 성취에 대해

02 You should be aware **of** danger **of** handling these explosives.
     당신은 알고 있어야 한다   위험에 대해   다루는 것의   이 폭발물들을

03 She placed the basket **of flowers on the table by the window**.
     그녀는 놓았다.   꽃바구니를   테이블 위에   창문 옆에

04 Choosing a right bike depends **on** what you want to use it for.
     올바른 자전거를 선택하는 것은 달려있다   네가 그것을 무엇을 위해 사용하는지에

05 He **is fond of** playing the piano for his fiancee.

06 The company **is interested in** establishing a charity for people in need.

07 The stricter attendance policy has **resulted in** fewer absences.

08 My daughter **belongs to** the debate team at school.

09 My little boy **insists on** taking his favorite toy truck with him every where he goes.

10 The flock of tiny swallows flew **over the trees near the lake**.

11 We have been looking forward **to returning** home.

12 Robert strongly objected **to the terms** of the contract.

13 The meeting will be devoted **to hearth** and safety issues.

4-7 재귀목적어

*재귀대명사가 강조로 사용되는 경우에는 "스스로"로 해석이 되지만 목적어 위치에 놓이게 되면 "자신을, 자신에게"로 해석이 됩니다.

01 I built this house **myself**. (강조: 생략 가능)

02 She cut **herself** on the glass. (목적어: 그녀는 유리에 베였다)

03 He poured **himself** a glass of cold water.

04 Sometimes it's hard for us to think of ourselves as adults.

05 You'll hurt yourself if you're not careful.

06 Teachers have no choice but to take **measures** to protect themselves. (수단, 조치)

07 The machine switches itself off when the process is complete.

08 I'm going to take Taekwondo lessons to learn how to defend myself.

09 If you want something done right, you'd better do it yourself. (강조)

10 Be true to yourself and know enough to walk away from temptation.

11 We must ensure that we do not set ourselves goals that are not attainable.

12 The government must commit itself to improving healthcare.

❖ 해석의 관건은 역시 어휘!!!

01 After we discussed our options, we decided on attending the play.

02 Sue is such an optimist that she makes everyone around her feel positive.

03 Everyone assumed that she was pregnant, but in fact, she was just overweight.

04 Detectives examined the dead body to see if there were any clues to the cause of death.

05 The professor said that we should become addicted to constant and never-ending self-improvement.

06 We guarantee that if you're not completely satisfied with our product, you'll get your money back.

07 A lot of writers find it difficult to earn a living from writing.

08 This function can make it easy to flip back and forth to different angles.

09 The actress and her spouse now dedicates themselves to children's charity work.

10 I declined, but she insisted on following me for several hundred yards.

11 Your devotion to your job is admirable, but remember, there are other things in life apart from work.

12 Police have found the body of an elderly man in an old abandoned car on a small dirt road in the countryside.

❖ **하고자 하는 의지력만 있어도 훌륭합니다!**

01 We elected the same candidate as we had done last time.

02 Green spaces have a calming effect, requiring less attention than busy city street does.

03 High school age kids will convince you that they don't care what you think, but they do.

04 Not only do the attitudes and healthy habits your close friends influence you, their relative success does, too.

05 Most people don't pay attention to what you look like. Even if they do, they won't remember at all.

06 The only jokes I tell are the ones that I hear from you.

07 Most bullies are the kids that other students look up to; the ones everybody wants to hang out with.

08 In ancient times, the rainbow was not only a symbol of the divine one but hope, peace, and victory.

09 Every day one is faced with situations which are not what they appear.

10 The first IMAX system displayed images of far greater size than those of the typical film.

11 There are many problems facing gamers. Among them, the most serious one is that they possibly don't know the real world from a false world.

12 **It is** not the style of clothes one wears, neither the kind of automobile one drives, nor the amount of money one has in the bank, **that** counts.

13 Most fat people don't eat proper food at a proper time. By doing so, they can reduce much of their weight in a short time.

❖ 모르면 해석이 안 되는 대동사

(A) 대동사: 앞에 나온 **동사의 반복을 피하기 위해 대신 사용하는 동사**로, do, does, did가 있고 원 동사 의미로 해석을 해야 한다.

01 He said this volcano would **erupt** soon, and it **did**.
그는 말했다 이 화산이 분출할 것이라고 곧, 그리고 그것은 분출 했다.

02 Every country in the western world **uses** more paper today than it **did** ten years ago.
모든 나라들은 서구 세계에서 사용 한다 더 많은 종이를 오늘날 그것 (모든 나라)이 10년 전 사용했던 것 보다

03 Last time you didn't **check** each door, but this time please **do** that for me.

04 She **beat** him in the swimming competition as she **had done** last year.

05 Many parents **compare** their **children** with other excellent **ones** though their children hate it when they **do**.

06 If you win or do well at something, Don't **show off**. If you **do**, people won't care about what talents you may have.

07 Not all of them believed that she **had stolen** my money, but one of those who **did** was Frank.

08 Teachers who prefer that children **see** beauty as they themselves **do** are not encouraging a sense of aesthetics in children.

09 Selfish adults or kids do not **make** sound decisions as well as **do** grateful people.

10 Every aspect of human language has evolved: as **have** components of the human brain and body, to engage in conversation and social life.

11 Winston Churchill was severly criticised in his days, just as most of our public figures **are**. (비교)

❖ 모르면 해석이 안 되는 대명사

(B) 대명사 one, ones, that, those (one morning, 어느 날 아침, one day, the other day)

01 **The population of** the United States is slightly more than twice **that of** Russia.
　　　인구는　　　　　미국의　　　　　약간 더 많다　　두 배 이상　러시아의 그것의

02 **The bus** was so crowded, we decided to take a later **one**.
　　버스는　　너무 혼잡해서　　우리는 나중에 것을(버스) 타기로 결심했다.

03 **One** can never be too careful in choosing a friend. (일반적인 사람)
　　사람은 아무리 조심해도 지나치지 않다　친구를 선택하는데 있어.

04 The older one is, the more emotionally mature **one** is.

05 If you take in too much water, like **one** who is drowning, it could kill you.

06 A good life is **the one** inspired by love and guided by knowledge.

07 The greatest mistake a man can make is to be afraid of making one.

08 There are several sightings throughout the years, but the most popular one took place last month.

09 The girl I talked with on the phone was more polite than the one I spoke with the other day.

10 The price of crude oil is not the only factor that contributes to the changes in that of gasoline.

11 In the 2002 Salt Lake City Games, the number of male athletes was more than twice that of female athletes.

12 It is important to wear short pants since long ones can cause accidents as they can get caught in the bike's wheels or chain.

13 Animals that are regularly disturbed by visitors are more likely to tolerate your intrusion than those that have had little previous contact with humans.

Chapter 2

Part 1. 동사 주어의 움직임이나 과정을 나타내는 말
She **goes** to work early.
It **has rained** for a week.

Part 2. 조동사 본동사에 어떤 보조적인 의미를 첨가하는 기능
He **may pass** the test.
We **should work** together.

Part 3. 수동태 주어가 어떤 동작의 대상이 되어 그 작용을 받는 서술형식
She **was invited** to the party.
It **was made of** cheese.

Part 4. 가정법 사실과 반대의 상황이나, 희망을 표현할 때 사용하는 문장
If I were you, I wouldn't do it.
I wish I had a son like you.

Part 1 동사

1. 현재시제와 현재진행

The earth **goes** around the sun.
She **is getting** married next week.

2. 현재완료와 현재완료진행

He **has been** happy since he got married.
We **have done** the dishes together.
It **has been raining** for 3 days.

3. 과거와 과거완료

I **made** a terrible mistake.
She **found** that he **had used** her computer.

4. 미래, 미래진행, 미래완료

I **will take** a nap.
She **will be talking** with John early tonight.
He **will have reached** New York tonight.

5. 한 지붕 두 가족 [한 문장에 두 개의 다른 시간 대]

She **seems to have been** to the shop.

1-1 현재시제와 현재 진행형

* 현재시간을 나타내는 경우: 주어의 **상태**나, **사실**, **습관**, **진리**를 나타내며, 현재진행형은 현재 진행 되는 경우와 가까운 미래에 반드시 발생하는 경우에 사용합니다.

01 Sometimes people **spread** others' private information accidentally. (사실)
사람들은 퍼트린다.   다른 사람들의 사생활정보를   우연히

02 You **reap** what you **sow**. (진리)
당신은 수확한다. 당신이 심은 것을 (뿌린 대로 거둔다)

03 This love, lasting forever, **makes** me immortal.

04 Parents **are** a child's most natural supporters and the best role models to learn from.

05 Sound waves **move** faster in warm air than in cold air.

06 Habits can even be the source of your happiness or the cause of your bitter cry.

07 The use of natural light makes consumers spend more money in stores.

08 Darwin believed that each generation of species is slightly different from the previous one.

09 Women are making up only a small proportion of the French population.

10 Our capacity for forgiveness is a triumph of the human spirit.

11 The merchant class is becoming increasingly important in many parts.

12 Some students are participating in community service to help those in need.

13 Certain things can happen and really get us down. That's a process we must all go through.

1-2 현재완료와 현재완료진행형

* 과거에 어떤 일이 발생하여 현재까지 관련된 일에 대해 표현하는 형태이며,
경험, 완료, 계속, 결과의 네 가지 용법으로 사용되고 have + 과거분사의 형태를 취합니다.
현재완료 진행형은 과거에 발생한 일이 지금도, 그리고 당분간 계속 진행되는 경우에 사용.

01 **The role of women has changed** since the revolution.
　　여성의 역할은　　　변화해 왔다　　　혁명이래로

02 She claims that she **has experienced** racism.
　　그녀는 주장한다　　　그녀가 인종차별을 경험한 적 있다고

03 I think you **have gone** too far. I mean you have crossed the line.

04 We **have appointed** a manager responsible for personal information.

05 They **have established** their own rules and regulations to maintain their position.

06 We should keep in mind that we have borrowed our planet from our future generations.

07 Solar energy in some countries has played an important role as energy resources.

08 Tuna has been in steady decline for years, victims of uncontrolled overfishing.

09 She has had steady effect on improving his capability in the field.

10 I **have been trying** to contact you but you seem to be very busy.

11 She has been showing constant effort to achieve her goal.

12 Studies of identical twins who have been raised apart / show that genes have a strong influence on one's weight.

1-3 과거와 과거완료 (had + p. p)

*과거에 **두 가지 일이 발생했을 때 더 먼저 발생한 것은 과거완료로 나중에 발생한 것은 과거로** 사용

> **01** When she **failed** it, she **needed** encouragement, not criticism. (과거 사실)
> 그녀가 그것을 실패했을 때, 그녀는 격려가 필요했다, 비난이 아니라
>
> **02** The inspector at the airport **examined** our baggage piece by piece.
> 공항의 검사원이 조사했다 우리의 짐을 하나하나
>
> **03** She **lost** the bag her mother **had bought** her on her birthday. (과거에 두 가지 일이 발생)
> 후에 발생 먼저 발생

04 The principal **restricted** class sizes to 20 students.

05 As the volcano in Iceland **erupted** for the first time in over 200 years, many people were terrified.

06 I **didn't go** to the movies because I **had seen** it several times before.

07 He exactly **recalled** who **had most contributed** to our society last year.

08 This country had been a colony of England before it declared its independence.

09 I noticed that the person had lost consciousness after being injured.

10 What made me upset was that she denied what she had said about the incident.

11 I was at a loss to find that I had got five tickets in the mail for illegal parking.

12 The government made a rule that no young man could marry until he had served a certain number of years in the army.

1-4 미래, 미래진행, 미래완료

*(will, be going to, will be / be going to be ~ing, will have p. p)

A 단순미래: I **will pass** the test.
I'**m going to meet** her tonight.

B 미래진행형: I'**m going to be watching** TV at 7 tomorrow evening.
나는 TV를 보고 있을 것이다.

C 미래완료: I **will have done** it early tonight.
나는 그것을 끝내게 될 것이다. 이른 저녁에

01 Some of our groups **will review** the effectiveness of the programs.

02 She **is going to get rid of** everything that she never uses.

03 We **will be making** every effort to satisfy our client's demand.

04 I'**m going to be distributing** food to the poor by the time you get here.

05 I **will have submitted** this application five times by next week.

06 He will be having a conversation with her teacher this time tomorrow.

07 I will be waiting for your reply tonight.

08 More people will have relied on the Internet for news.

09 You will have done it 100 times by constant repetition by this afternoon.

10 She will have interviewed 20 applicants according to the schedule.

1-5 한 지붕 두 가족 (한 문장에서 두 개의 다른 시간대가 존재하는 경우)

01 She **seems to have lost interest** in me. *더 먼저 발생한 것은 완료형으로 표시
그녀는   나에게 관심을 잃은 것처럼 보인다.

It seems that she **has lost or lost** interest in me. (현재완료 혹은 과거 둘 다 가능)

02 I **was** proud of **having worked** for the company until my retirement.
나는 자랑스럽다   일한 것에 대해   회사에서   나의 은퇴까지

= I was proud that I **had worked** for the company until my retirement.

03 The birthstones **are** thought to **have originated** in Poland.

04 Hippocrates **is said** to **have written** the Hippocratic Oath, which is a promise that doctors have to keep.

05 Mike **appears** to **have been** kidnapped by someone we know.

06 She **regrets** not **having selected** a proper color for the product.

07 He admits to having battled self-confidence issues for his whole life.

08 Wrinkles on jacket were caused by her having worn it.

09 Harry was the only person to have survived the tragic battle.

10 They didn't seem to have had much trouble getting work.

11 Ten people were reported to have lost their lives in the crash.

12 Having felt ashamed of what I did, I sent her a letter of apology.

13 Not having been satisfied, I will claim compensation.

CHECK POINT 7

❖ **어라, 해석이 잘 되기 시작한다.**

01 The Winter Festival is an annual event at our school.

02 As you know, every problem contains the seeds of its own solution.

03 The students were anxiously waiting for the results of their final exam.

04 Your son has been consistently late for class for the last two weeks.

05 They abandoned the dog because they could no longer take care of it.

06 The police made a thorough search of the area but were unable to find the escaped prisoner.

07 Mark hadn't sufficiently cleaned the carpet, so we could still see the wine stains.

08 The patient explained the symptoms she had experienced to her doctor.

09 You will be experiencing malnutrition when you don't eat enough amounts of the right food.

10 The researchers will have conducted all the experiments by this Friday.

11 Having been to the ruins in Italy, I can recommend a few good places to visit.

12 The unique blend of experience of mine has made me a woman with an original point of view and a broader mind to life.

Part 2 조동사

* 조동사는 동사를 도와 동사에 부가적인 의미를 더 하는 역할을 하며 조동사 다음에는 항상 동사 원형만 사용된다.

1. 내가 아직도 모르는 can의 의미!

You can be a chooser.
I can't attend the class.

2. may와 might는 brother야!

She may be a teacher.
This might not happen again.

3. must는 알겠는데 can't 너는 누구니?

She must be tired of living alone.
He can't be a teacher.

4. should, ought to는 이란성 쌍둥이

We should keep the rules.
I ought not to change the plan.

5. 조동사 과거는 형태가 다 같아요?

He may have been sick yesterday.
They must have had a good time.

6. 주관적인 의견의 should

I ask that he stay healthy.
It is natural that we protect nature.

7. 나도 조동사야!

I used to eat instant food.
She would rather live alone.

2-1 내가 아직도 모르는 can의 의미가 있다고?

＊can: ~할 수 있다와 ~해도 된다. 그리고 ~일 수도 있다. 라고 해석.
　could 또한 can의 과거로 사용되기도 하지만 현재시간대로 ~일 수도 있다. 로의 의미로 사용한다.

01 Watching TV **can help interact** with other cultures.
　　　TV를 보는 것은　　도와줄 수 있다 교류하도록 (능력) 다른 문화들과

02 Sometimes, problems **can appear** to be unsolvable.
　　　때때로,　　　문제들은 해결될 수 없는 것처럼 보일 수 있다. (가능성)

03 River boundaries **can change** as rivers change course.

04 I **can't wait** to start a new day.

05 Drinking water **can contribute** to good health.

06 You can buy conditions for happiness, but you can't buy happiness.

07 It can be tough to settle down to study when there are so many distractions.

08 If you want to join the expedition, you must be able to speak Spanish.

09 Most accidents in the home **could be prevented**.(현재 가능한 추측)

10 Very old trees in particular can offer clues about what the climate was like.

11 Bad lighting can increase stress on your eyes, as can light that is too bright, or light that shines directly into your eyes.

2-2 may와 might는 brother야!

* may와 might는 거의 같은 동의어로 사용되지만 (~일지도 모른다, ~해도 된다.)
  허락인 경우 may를 주로 사용한다.

01 Evaluation **may motivate** them to work harder next time.
　　　평가는 동기부여할지도 모른다　　　그들을 더 열심히 공부하도록 다음에

02 Someone lonely **might benefit** from helping others.
　　　외로운 사람은　　혜택을 받을지도 모른다 다른 사람들을 돕는 것으로부터

03 We have a set of rules to show what you **may** and may not do.

04 It **might** be a good idea to put those plants in the shade.

05 People taking vitamin C every day **may** be more health-conscious overall.

06 The construction might lead to increased traffic along the main street.

07 If teachers are not strict, many students might show a tendency to break the rules at school.

08 Adequate hydration may improve cognitive function among children and adolescents.

09 The minimum wage laws may be the only way to prevent many employees from working at wages that are below the poverty line.

10 Giving excessive rewards might have a negative effect on the attitude of the people doing the work.

11 Of the many forest plants that can cause poisoning, wild mushrooms may be among the most dangerous.

2-3 must는 알겠는데 can't 너는 누구니?

* must와 have to는 ~해야 한다의 의미와 ~임에 틀림없다. 가 있으며,
  can't가 추측으로 사용되는 경우에 must와 반대의미인 ~일 리가 없다의 의미를 가진다.
  don't have to / don't need to / need not: ~하지 않아도 된다의 의미를 가지고 있다.

01 You **must demand** your right to vote as a citizen.
　　　당신은 요구해야한다　당신의 권리를　투표 할　시민으로써

02 It is a huge building, so you **can't miss it**.
　　　그것은 큰 건물이다,　그래서 당신은 그것을 놓칠 리가 없다. (못 찾을 리가 없다)

03 A whale **must** come to the surface to breathe.

04 What he said about her **can't be true**.

05 Salmon **have to travel** upstream to lay their eggs.

06 Money is something you will have to deal with for the rest of your life.

07 You must bear certain pains and sorrows, because they will make you a better person.

08 Clothing doesn't have to be expensive to provide comfort during exercise.

09 In a new environment or area, we have to adapt and learn to perform in new ways.

10 You don't have to offend generous people who want to give some money for your help.

11 As consumers we just have to use our own judgment and avoid taking advertising claims too seriously.

2-4 should, ought to는 이란성 쌍둥이!!!

* 당연한 일에 대해서 언급하는 경우에 가장 많이 사용되며, 상대방에 대한 충고나 조언등 바라는 일이 이뤄지기를 희망하는 의미에서 사용되며, ought to는 should와 같은 의미이지만 매우 형식적인 표현에만 사용된다.

01 You **should overcome** a lot of difficulties to get where you want to be.
　　　극복해야 한다　　　많은 역경들을　　도달하기 위해 네가 있기를 원하는 곳에

02 Many Americans think that America **ought not to take part in** the war.
　　　많은 미국인들은 생각한다　　미국이　　　참여해서는 안 된다고 전쟁에

03 We **should hire** some temporary office help during this busy time.

04 You **shouldn't be** too pessimistic at what you do.

05 This is exactly the same kind of information we **ought to ignore**.

06 The government should restrict tobacco advertising on TV.

07 People should be held responsible for posting comments on the Internet.

08 What if I should fall sick and not be able to work?

09 If you show the receipt, there ought not to be any difficulty getting your money back.

10 The courts ought to treat black and white defendants in exactly the same way.

11 They can just be people who believe they ought to reshape society from top to bottom.

CHECK POINT 8

❖ **가끔은 꼼꼼한 해석이 필요한 경우도 있다.**

01 If Mike likes you, he will do anything that he can to please you.

02 Many kids with mechanical tendencies can't resist the desire to take their bike apart!

03 You might be used to a busy schedule, but keeping busy all the time could lead to trouble.

04 As our ability to control genes improves, parents may be able to design their own children.

05 Production costs must not exceed more than $1,000.

06 This jewel can't be fake. I bought it from a jewelry collector.

07 You ought not to reveal your emotions when you are upset.

08 Students must highlight the strengths and talents that make them unique.

09 We might not have to hear your interpretation of the current political situation.

10 We should know that the root cause of cyber violence is the fact that Internet users are not communicating.

11 What may surprise you even more is there are many stars in the universe that are thousands of times hotter than the sun.

12 The low number of people attending the lecture must be a clear indication of lack of interest in the topic.

2-5 조동사 과거는 형태가 다 같은가?

(A) may have p. p / might have p. p: ~ 했을지도 모른다.
(B) must have p. p: ~ 했음이 틀림없다 / can't have p. p: ~ 였을 리가 없다.
(C) should have p. p: ~했어야만 했는데 (과거 사실에 대한 후회나 비판)

＊추측에 관한 조동사의 과거는 **조동사 다음에 have p.p**

01 He **may have replaced** the batteries in my bicycle light because it's not dim.
대체했을지도 모른다.   건전지를   나의 자전거 전등에   왜냐하면 그것이 흐리지 않기 때문에

02 Jenny **can't have admitted her fault**. She still thinks she didn't do anything wrong.
그녀의 잘못을 인정했을 리가 없다.   그녀는 여전히 생각한다 그녀가 잘못한 것이 없다고

03 You **must have heard of the proverb**, 'Birds of a feather flock together.'
속담에 대해 들었음에 틀림없다   유유상종

04 I **should have apologized to you** for waking you up last night.
사과했어야만 했는데   너에게   너를 깨운 것에 대해 지난밤에

05 She **might have been** unaware of the problem until it got worse.

06 He **must have pretended** to like her opinion to avoid an argument.

07 She **can't have driven** her car. Her car keys are still here

08 You **shouldn't have made** threats against your neighbor. You could have been arrested.

09 The applicant must have forgotten to attach his photo to the resume.

10 The manager said nothing, and the meeting may have ended without any noteworthy changes.

11 The driver of the car can't have been conscious when the police arrived at the scene of the accident.

12 You might have gotten an ice cream headache-short, sharp, and awful pain in your head!

13 I should have dedicated myself to what I wanted to pursue.

2-6 이런 것도 알아야 주관적인 의견에 관한 표현 should

＊주절에 제안, 주장, 명령, 요구, 요청, 추천, 충고 등을 의미하는 동사나 형용사가 나오는 경우
that 이하에 주어 + [should] + 동사원형, should는 생략 가능하지만 뜻은 남는다.

(v) suggest / insist / order, command / demand, require / ask, request / recommend / advise
(a) natural / essential / necessary / imperative 등의 형용사 혹은 명사도 가능

01 It is **natural** that those who have a good habit **should succeed** in life. (주관적인 생각)
　　당연하다　　　　좋은 습관을 가진 사람들이　　　　성공하는 것은　　　삶에서

　　　　　　　　　　should가 생략되었으므로 동사원형
02 We suggested that Mike ∨ **change** his attitude. (Mike가 바꾼다? → 바꿔야한다.)
　　우리는 제안했다　　　Mike가 바꿔야 한다고 그의 태도를

03 Susie asked that he **find** healthier ways to relieve his stress.

04 She insisted that he **do** the work as it was supposed to be done.

05 The manager demanded that negative aspects also **be evaluated**.

06 We advised that teachers adopt a new approach in education.

07 The doctor suggested that Susie go for tests to find out what is causing her severe headaches.

08 It is essential that you attend next week's management meeting.

09 It is recommended that you always boil your water when you go wilderness camping.

10 It is imperative that the wounded be taken to the nearest hospital right now.

11 The evidence suggests that single fathers **are** more likely to work than single mothers. (객관적)

2-7 나도 조동사인데!!!

A **can't ~ too**: 아무리 ~해도 지나치지 않는
B **would rather**: 차라리 ~하는 것이 더 낫다.
C **used to**: ~하곤 했다 (과거에만)
D **would**: ~하곤 했다 (과거를 회상)
E **had better (may, might as well)**: ~하는 편이 낫다

---

01 You **can't be too careful** in choosing your friends.
너는 아무리 조심해도 지나치지 않다   고르는데 있어   너의 친구를

02 I **would rather keep silent** than reveal my emotions.
나는 차라리 침묵을 지키는 편이 낫다.   드러내는 것 보다 나의 감정을

03 He **used to bring** me roses when we had a date.
그는 가져다주곤 했다 나에게 장미를   우리가 데이트 할 때

04 When we worked in the same office, we **would often have** coffee together.
우리가 같은 사무실에 있었을 때   종종 커피를 마시곤 했다.

---

05 You **had better** not keep company with him. He is a trouble-maker.

06 She is not what she **used to** be.

07 I **would rather** not see her than apologize to her.

08 We can't know too much about the language we speak every day.

09 You can never have too much education or knowledge.

10 We're eating out more often than we used to.

11 I would rather taste ash on my tongue than blood in my mouth.

12 If there's nothing more to do, we may as well go to bed.

❖ **해석이냐 독해냐? 그것이 문제로다.**

01 This product can't have been manufactured in my factory. The logo is not right.

02 The soccer game must have temporarily been interrupted by a sudden, short downpour of rain.

03 They should have rewarded him with a free ticket.

04 They must have had some kind of ceremony every year at harvest time.

05 They might have demonstrated how to handle modern, high performance cars.

06 I would rather give up healing those patients. It is too hopeless.

07 She requires that we not neglect to do our duty.

08 I should have realized a man of your modesty would find such a question embarrassing.

09 Native tribes used to inhabit this island over 4,000 years ago.

10 You can't be too careful when it comes to taking financial advice.

11 The American children in colonial times might have had only one set of clothes and no shoes.

12 In order to improve balance and strength in the legs, I suggest you take up the slow-motion exercise combining flexibility and lower body strength.

13 We should stop sacrificing everything we want to do for a later promise of happiness, and simply live in the present instead.

Part 3 수동태

*주어에게 동작이 가해지는 경우 사용 되며, 주어가 ~이 되다. 로 해석이 되고, 문장 맨 뒤에 행위자를 알리는 by+목적격이 나오지만 실제 수동태는 누가 했는지 아는 경우와, 전혀 모르는 경우에 많이 사용 됩니다.

1. 일반적인 수동태, 그리고 3,4형식

She **was invited** to the party.
I **was sent** a gift.

2. 주어 보충어

The door **was painted green**.
Mike **was made to leave**.

3. 조동사가 등장하는 수동태

She **may be taken** to the hospital.
This cake **must be kept** in the ice box.

4. 시간대와 유형이 다른 수동태

She **has been given** many chances so far.

5. to-부정사, 동명사 수동태

I want him **to be punished** right now.
She is afraid of **being caught** in traffic.

6. by가 없어도 되는 수동태

This cake **is made of** cheese.
He **was known** as a kick boxing fighter.

7. 감정의 동사가 수동이 되는 경우

I **was satisfied** with your performance.
We **were excited** to be here

3-1 수동태의 형식은 be+p.p (주어에게 동작이 가해지는 경우에 사용한다)

01 Tea and biscuits **are provided** for guests.
　　　　　　　　　　제공 되어 진다

02 Water and salt **are quickly absorbed** into our blood stream.
　　　물과 소금은　　　　재빠르게 흡수 된다　　　　우리의 혈류로

03 Your bag **is left** as it was.
　　　당신의 가방은 남겨져 있다 그것이 있었던 그대로

04 Consumers **are more motivated** by friends' recommendations than by advertisements.

05 The ancient city **was destroyed** and buried during a long eruption of the volcano.

06 Winds in one region are always accompanied by different winds in another.

07 The car was assembled in less than two hours.

08 A great deal of meaning is conveyed by a few well-chosen words.

09 Waste materials are disposed of in a variety of ways.

＊3 ~ 4형식 수동태

10 Jenny **was given a beautiful antique ring** for her engagement.
　　　　　　주어졌다 (받았다) 아름다운 골동품 반지를

11 She **was asked** a few private questions by her boss.

12 We **were shown** a couple of masterpieces by Michelangelo.

13 The leather jacket was bought for me on my birthday.

14 Mike was offered another decent job, but he rejected it.

3-2 주어 보충어 (5형식이 수동태가 되면 2형식이 된다)

* 명사, 형용사 또는 to-부정사, 동명사가 수동태 다음에 나와 주어를 설명하거나 주어가 하는 동작을 나타내는 경우.

01 The meat is kept **cold** for later use.
　　고기는　　보관 된다 차갑게　나중에 사용을 위해

02 When water alone is **used to remove oil**, water will simply sit on top of it in a bubble.
　　단지 물만　　　　사용될 때 기름을 제거하기 위해,　　물은 단지 머무를 것이다 기름의 위에 거품으로

03 She was made **to agree** to the plan.
　　　　강요받았다　　동의하도록

04 He **was found guilty**, but he kept insisting he was innocent.

05 Many questions **were left unanswered** even after the class.

06 The rules **are considered too strict** for the children.

07 Some birds are seen migrating to the north at this time of year.

08 Mike was made to pursue his goal without hesitation by his coach.

09 The treatment was found very helpful for certain patients.

10 Dieters are often told to eat with chopsticks to avoid eating more.

11 Most children are used to reading fables illustrated with many interesting pictures.

12 Many doctors were contributed to keeping the virus from spreading out.

13 The measure is designed to protect workers from suffering from secondhand smoke.

3-3 조동사가 등장하는 수동태

*조동사 + be + p. p

> **01** The heavy containers **will be carried** by a few laborers.
> 　　　무거운 컨테이너는　　　　　　운반될 것이다　　　몇 명의 노동자에 의해
>
> **02** Your health **can be maintained** only by regular exercise and proper food.
> 　　　너의 건강은　　　유지될 수 있다　　　　단지 규칙적인 운동과 적절한 음식에 의해

03 How **can** this extraordinary difference in development **be explained**?

04 A recent photo **should be attached** to your application form.

05 30 **should be subtracted** from 45, then you will get 15.

06 Our reading club is a place where extreme political views can be expressed openly.

07 Your duty will be clearly defined by your supervisor.

08 It's well known that bugs should be fixed as soon as possible after they're identified.

09 Nutrients from the digested food in the stomach can be absorbed directly into the blood.

10 Poverty can be got rid of by efforts of the rich.

11 New technology must be applied to almost every industrial process.

12 Democracy might be expected to collapse under such pressure.

3-4 시간대 별 수동태와 그 외 형태

> **01** He **has been released** from prison to receive a medical treatment in Seoul. (현재완료 수동)
>   풀려났다   감옥으로부터   받기 위해 의료치료를 서울에서
>
> **02** It **is said** that she plays a huge role in her company.
>   ~라고 한다   그녀는 중요한 역할을 한다고 한다.   그녀의 회사에서
>   = She is said to play a huge role in her company.

03 She **was laughed at by** her friends for doing some stupid things.

04 I **have been frustrated** by my inability to stop the opposition forces.

05 She **has been dedicated** to conserving energy for the future generation.

06 Some grain has been associated with the wedding ceremony in ancient times.

07 The disabled often have been isolated and not permitted to participate in the normal course of life.

08 She was overwhelmed by his bold act which no one could even do.

09 It was declared at the conference that human dignity comes first.

10 Trees are always being hit by lightning, but seldom more than once because they get knocked down.

11 Companies are legally required to keep records of all their financial transactions.

12 You will be met on arrival at the airport and transferred to your hotel.

3-5 to-부정사, 동명사 수동태

* to + be + p. p / being + p. p

01 Illegal activities **are likely to be done** by everyone in a society.
불법적인 활동들은　　　　행하여 질 것 같다　　　모든 사람에 의해　한 사회에서

02 I felt like **being myself watched** yesterday.
나는　　　감시당하고 있는 것처럼 느꼈다.

03 I was lucky **to be selected** as a favorite professor at the college.

04 Our feelings about **being touched** also depend on our cultural background.

05 Silence is likely **to be interpreted** as lack of interest, unwillingness to communicate.

06 The rest of its body seems **to be covered** in many long feathers.

07 Wanting to be accepted by others is part of human nature.

08 The fishers have to avoid being eaten by killer whales and polar bears.

09 The disease being transferred from animals to humans is likely to happen.

10 Being severely focused on something makes us enter a *hypnotic state. (최면상태)

11 After being torn into very small thin pieces, old money is used to make new things.

12 Live the life you want to live by doing what needs to be done.

3-6 by가 필요 없는 수동태 필수 문장

01 Her music **was composed of** a complicated melody.
그녀의 음악은　　작곡 (구성) 되어있다　　　복잡한 멜로디로

02 Almost 80% of the population of Laos **are engaged in** agriculture.
　　　라오스 인구의 거의 80%는　　　　　　종사한다

03 I **was** involuntarily **involved in** a constant dispute with my neighbors.
　　나는 비자발적으로　　관련되었다　　끊임없는 분쟁에　　나의 이웃사람들과

04 His theory in economics **is not related to** a current trend.
　　경제학에서의 그의 이론은　　　관련이 없다.　　현재의 경향과

05 My complaint **was referred to** the manufacturers and they will send me new products.

06 Hard labor should **be associated with** high earnings.

07 We should **be concerned about** the quality of life we live.

08 Some sports are so expensive that participation **is** largely **limited to** wealthy people.

09 The committee **is made up of** representatives from every state.

10 Fever **is** usually **defined** as an oral temperature above 37.4 degrees.

11 Compulsive shopping is a serious disorder that can ruin lives if **it's** not recognized and treated.

12 The professor **was accused of** stealing his student's ideas and publishing them.

13 Many politicians **are** more **concerned with** power and control than with the good of the people.

14 In Korea, Education levels **are** strongly **related to** income.

3-7 감정을 표현하는 동사가 분사가 되면!

* 감정을 나타내는 동사가 과거분사의 형태인 수동형이 되더라도 해석은 능동으로 하며, 꾸며주는 대상이 감정을 일으키게 하는 경우에는 현재분사를 사용합니다.

> disappoint: 실망시키다 ⇨ disappointed: 실망한 ⇨ disappointing: 실망스런
> embarrass: 당황하게 하다 ⇨ embarrassed: 당황한 ⇨ embarrassing: 당황스런

01 She passed out when she heard **shocking news** about her son.

02 He **became interested** in biology while attending a technical school and enrolled in medical school.

03 Margot **gets irritated** if people leave dirty dishes in the sink.

04 A lot of people eat too much when they're depressed.

05 He was frightened to be kidnapped when was left alone.

06 Her mother was pleased that she chose a college close to home.

07 When we are annoyed with ourselves, it means that we have high expectations of ourselves.

08 She had become increasingly frustrated with her life.

09 He gets frustrated when people don't understand what he is trying to say

10 If you're not completely satisfied, you can get your money back.

11 I was relieved to find out that Jake was generous enough to forgive me for what I said.

CHECK POINT 10

❖ **해석을 하다 막히면 내가 무엇이 부족한지 생각해 보자!!!**

01 Rising sea levels are linked to global warming and some islands could sink into the sea.

02 In the real world we are constantly, consciously, and unconsciously exposed to public ads.

03 Nothing of importance was ever achieved by an individual acting alone.

04 He has been known as a suspect of the robbery.

05 Genetics explains how certain characteristics are passed on from parents to children.

06 She was depressed at the sight of the people suffering poverty.

07 We are encouraged to define ourselves and obtain others' approval by acquiring possessions.

08 It is said that the rise in crime is related to an increase in unemployment rate.

09 Many people are concerned about the declining number of speakers of their own language.

10 When starting my pond, I was overwhelmed by the generosity of friends and neighbours with all sorts of pond plants.

11 As long as exposure to radiation is carefully controlled, life expectancy will be prolonged rather than destroyed.

12 Researchers found that women who were depressed recovered much more quickly according to the number of times they were hugged and the duration of those hugs.

Part 4 가정법

*가정법은 동사의 시제에 따라 **상황에 반대되는 경우를 표현할 때** 사용합니다.

0 If 문장에서 동사가 **현재형**이 나오는 경우는 **현재 발생할 가능성이 50%**인 경우를 말합니다. (조건문)

* If she **comes** home late, mom will be angry. (가능성이 반반)

1 If 문장에서 동사가 **과거형**이 나오면 가정법이라 하고 **현재 사실에 대한 반대 경우**를 표현합니다.

* If I **had** some money, I would lend you some. (현재 가능성이 전혀 없는 경우)

2 If 문장에서 동사가 **과거완료 형태**가 나오면 **과거사실의 반대 되는 경우**를 표현 할 때

* If I **had not been busy, I would have visited** you. (과거 사실의 반대 상황)

3 혼합 가정법 If 문장은 과거사실의 반대이고, 주절 문장은 현재 사실의 반대되는 경우를 표현할 때

* If he had been more careful, he wouldn't be at the hospital now.
* If she had gone on a diet last year, she would be slender by now.

4 미래 가능성이 희박한 should, 가능성이 전혀 없는 were to

* If she were to be born again, she would marry you.

5 ~이 없다면 if it were not for, ~이 없었더라면 if it had not been for

If it were not for your help, If it hadn't been for your help,

6 I wish I **had** some free time. (~라면 좋을텐데)

I wish I **had not been** busy. (~였다면 좋을텐데)

7 나도 가정법이야!!!

as if, as though, otherwise

4-1 가정법 과거 (If + 주어 + 과거동사, 주어 + would, could, might + 동사원형)

* 과거 동사가 현재 사실의 반대를 나타냄 : ~일 텐데, ~할 수 있을 텐데, ~일지도 모르는데

01 What **would** you do if you **were** in my shoes? (be동사가 나오면 인칭에 관계없이 were)
    어떻게 하겠니?   만약에 당신이 나의 입장이라면

02 If I **got** another chance, I **could make** it. (기회가 주어지지 않는 상황)
    만약에 내가 또 다른 기회를 얻는다면, 나는 해낼 수 있는데

03 If she **apologized** to me, I **would** forgive her.

04 If she **didn't try** to compete in the tryout, her dream **would never** come true.

05 What **would happen** if you only **saved** your money and never spent it?

06 Robin could lead a healthier life if she gave up smoking.

07 If I were in your shoes, I would not take part in the contest.

08 If someone offered me a job in another country, I would accept it right away.

09 If I inherited billion dollars, I would travel to the moon.

10 If I had a demanding job, I would give up and find another one.

11 If his liver functioned properly, it would distribute chemicals produced by the digestive system.

12 I'd be happy to keep my own garden to grow some food, if only I had the space for one.

13 If you could endure the intense heat of the desert during the journey, you would get to the destination safely.

4-2 가정법 과거완료 (If + 주어 + had + p. p, 주어 + would, could, might + have p. p)

✱ 과거완료 형태가 과거 사실의 반대 상황을 나타냄

01 If the soldier **had gone** one step farther, he **might have fallen** to either injury or death.
만약에 그 병사가 한 발짝만 더 갔더라면, 그는 부상당하거나 죽게 되었을지도 모른다.

02 If you **had gotten** some financial advice, you **wouldn't have gone** bankrupt.
만약에 네가 재정적인 조언을 받았었더라면, 너는 파산하지 않았을 텐데.

03 My injuries **would have been worse** if I **hadn't been wearing** my bicycle helmet.

04 If we **had prepared** a little earlier, our performance **could have exceeded** their expectation.

05 If someone **had offered** me a ride, I **might have gone** to the concert.

06 If they had had more lifeboats on board, more passengers would have been saved.

07 If that guy had given me the correct directions, then I wouldn't have met my wife.

08 If the king had conquered the territory, his descendants would have settled down there.

09 If she hadn't insisted on going to the concert, we would have saved a lot more money.

✱ 혼합 가정법 (If는 과거사실의 반대, 주절은 현재사실의 반대)

01 If we **had looked at** the map, we **wouldn't be lost.**
지도를 봤었더라면 길을 잃지 않을 텐데.

02 If I **had practiced** more, I **would have** a driver's license now.
만약에 내가 연습을 더 했더라면 나는 지금 운전 면허증을 가지고 있을 텐데.

03 If I **hadn't driven** a car, I **would be** in Paris now.

04 If your illness **hadn't healed**, I **would be concerned** about you.

4-3 미래 가능성이 희박한 should

∗ should 그럴 일은 없겠지만, 전혀 없는 were to

01 If the sun **were to rise** in the west tomorrow, she would be here on time.
　　만약에 내일 해가 서쪽에서 뜬다면　　　　　　　그녀가 제 시간에 올 것이다.

02 If it **should** rain tomorrow,　I will (would) stay home.
　　만약에 내일 비가 온다면, (비가 올 일은 없겠지만) 나는 집에 있을 것이다.

03 If he **should be struck** by a bolt of lightning, we **wouldn't be surprised**.

04 If you **were to place** a glass in a pan of water and heat the water slowly, all the surfaces of the glass **would expand** evenly, making the whole glass a little bigger.

∗ ~이 없다면, ~이 없었더라면

05 **If it were not for** the college degree, he would have a hard time finding a job.
　　Without (But for) 대학 학위가 없다면,　　　　　그는 직업을 찾느라 고생할 텐데.

06 **If it had not been for** the revolution, the role of women wouldn't have changed.
　　Without　　　　　혁명이 없었더라면,　　　　여성의 역할은 변화하지 않았을 텐데.

07 **If it were not for** the natural instinct, wildlife couldn't survive.

08 **If it had not been for** a close examination, two contrary views wouldn't emerge easily now.

∗ If가 생략되면 주어+동사가 → 동사+주어로 (도치)

09 **Were it not for** your help, I wouldn't achieve anything.
　　If it were not for your help,

10 **Had it not been for** your help, what could I have done?
　　If it had not been for

4-4 I wish (현재나 과거의 이루어 질 수 없는 소망이나 바람을 표현)

01 I **wish** I were wealthy enough to buy a house on the hill. (가정법 과거)
내가 부유하다면 좋을 텐데

02 I **wish** I **had had** more time to study for the test. (가정법 과거완료)
내가 시간이 더 많았더라면 좋았을 텐데.

03 I wish he **could be aware** of the fact that I am on his side.

04 I wish my parents **could adjust** to living in an apartment.

05 I wish Mike didn't distract the other students during class.

06 I wish the speech were broadcast live with simultaneous translation.

07 I wish I **had been born** with a silver spoon in my month.

08 I wish you **had known** that you had a obligation to finish her mission.

09 I wish she hadn't concealed the fact that she was pregnant.

10 I wish I had received wise advice from those with more life experience than I had.

11 I wish she had been perceived as a future chief executive.

12 I wish the city had imposed a ban on smoking in all public places.

13 I wish I had known that certain forms of mental illness can be triggered by food allergies.

4-5 가지가지 가정법 (if가 없어도 가정법, 혹은 다른 의미를 가진 가정법)

01 The close examination of the proof **might have brought** a good result.
증거의 면밀한 조사는　　　　　　　　　　가져왔을지도 모른다.　　　　좋은 결과를

02 I took her out of the road, otherwise she **would have been run over** by a truck.
나는 그녀를 도로에서 끌어냈다.　　　　그렇지 않았더라면 그녀는 트럭에 의해 치였을 텐데.

03 What could I have done **without** you?

04 The landlord treats me **as if I were** his son, not a tenant. (마치 ~인 것처럼)

05 **Suppose** you **were trapped** on a desert island with no sources of fresh water, what would you do?(=If)

06 Jenny was behaving **as if** (= as though) there were great contrasts between them.

07 **Should** you need any help (=if you need any help), you can always phone me at the office. (=If)

08 **Even if** she survived, she would never fully recover. (설사 ~일지라도)

09 They got two free tickets to Canada, **otherwise** they'd never have been able to afford to go.

10 The government officials talked as if they had coped with natural disasters efficiently.

11 People can actually end up appearing more foolish when they act as if they had knowledge that they do not.

12 When students evaluate their teachers, valuable feedback can be gathered which would otherwise be lost.

13 Almost everyone feels that his or her own opinion is a good one, otherwise he or she wouldn't be sharing it with you.

❖ 중요한 것은 바로 시간이지!!!

01 If I had someone to replace you, I would let you go to London.

02 If I were you, I would keep her as my constant companion.

03 I wish she could resist the temptation to have a plastic surgery.

04 I wish my boss wouldn't always arrange the meetings during lunch time.

05 Musical ideas sprang into his head, fully formed, as if he were taking dictation.

06 His smile was as though a brilliant light had illuminated the dim ballroom.

07 If he had shown us great talent, he would have stayed attractive to us.

08 If the roads hadn't been so slippery, I wouldn't have had an accident.

09 If he had expanded his business into Europe, he would have been more successful.

10 If his passport had not expired, he would be in the airplane now.

11 She stared at me as though I were a complete stranger.

12 If he hadn't invested in stocks, he wouldn't have gone bankrupt.

13 If I were to lie about my age on grounds of vanity, and my lying were discovered, even though no serious harm would have been done, I would have undermined your trust generally.

❖ 모르면 해석이 안 되는 필수 어휘

(A) 부정표현 not은 never 등의 부정어와 같이 사용할 수 없다.

hardly, seldom, rarely, scarcely, barely [거의 ~이 아닌] * barely [간신히 ~한]

01 She could hardly eat anything because of her sore throat.

02 Trees are always being hit by lightning, but seldom more than once because they get knocked down!

03 She is loved and visited by many, and is rarely alone.

04 It was getting dark and he could scarcely see in front of him.

05 She was barely aware of his presence. * I thought I would fail but I barely made it.

(B) few + 셀 수 있는 명사 / little + 셀 수 없는 명사 [거의 없는] a few [몇] a little [약간, 작은]

01 She is so selfish that she has few friends around her. [동사를 부정어로 해석 한다]

02 Few things can be discussed right now.

03 Until the invention of the electric light bulb, they had little choice but to sleep a lot.

04 He has little money left for the trip because he wasted too much on clothes.

(C) 부분 부정 (all, every, both, always, necessarily) + not과 함께 사용되면 **~인 것은 아니다**. 로 해석

01 The rich are not always happy.
    부자들이 항상 행복한 것은 아니다.

02 All of them don't have enough for food.

03 Not both of them agreed to your plan.

04 Having this disease does not necessarily mean that you will die young.

딱!
한권으로 정리되는
구문독해

Chapter 3

Part 1. **원인과 결과를 나타내는 구문 & 문장**

Part 2. **목적을 나타내는 구 & 문장**

Part 3. **분사 구문**

Part 1 이유, 원인과 결과를 나타내는 구문 & 문장 모두

(A) 감정을 나타내는 형용사 다음에 to-부정사가 나오면 **~해서, ~ 때문에** 라고 해석

(B) live, grow, awake (wake) 다음에 to-부정사가 **and의 의미**를 갖는다.

(C) 형용사 다음에 to-부정사가 나오면 **~하기가, 하기에** 라고 해석을 한다.

---

01 She **is excited to shoot** a film with Tom Cruise.
(감정의 형용사) 신이난다 / 영화를 찍게 되어서

　* Mike **was surprised that her father bought him a car**.
　　　　　　놀랬다　　　　　　그의 아버지가 그에게 차를 사줘서

02 He grew up **to** be a lawyer. (and의 의미)
　　그는 자라서 변호사가 되었다.

03 His behavior is **hard** for us **to predict**. (형용사 hard를 꾸며주는 역할)
　　그의 행동은　　　어렵다　우리가 예측하기가

---

04 She is not easy **to please**.

05 Have you ever woken up **to** find yourself in a hospital?

06 I am sad **to inform** you that you can no longer be with us.

07 I am happy to get the job which I applied for.

08 He arrived there to find that the last train had already left.

09 I felt disappointed to find that the rate only applies to purchases.

10 Some customers are quite difficult to handle.

11 I was deeply embarrassed to see my sister arrive in a very short skirt.

(D) too ~ to 너무나 ~해서 ~할 수가 없다 (부정의 의미)   so ~ that s+ [can't]
(E) 형용사 enough + to-부정사 + ~할 정도로 ~하다   so ~ that s+ [can] / such ~ that

01 She was **too** excited **to** calm down.
그녀는 너무나 신이 나서 진정할 수 없었다.

02 John was **so bored that he couldn't help but fall asleep**.
너무나 지루해서   그는 잘 수밖에 없었다.

03 He is **such** an idiot **that** no one wants to be his friend.
너무 멍청해서   아무도 그의 친구가 되고 싶지 않다.

04 You will be old **enough to** vote in election.

05 The knight was brave **enough to** cut off the dragon's head with his magic sword.

06 She is emotionally mature and financially stable **enough to** cope with difficult situations.

07 No one is ever **too** grown-up **to** cry.

08 Time is too precious to spend on worthless things.

09 Everything happened **so** quickly **that** I didn't have time to think.

10 Her achievements were so great that everyone sincerely admired him.

11 Stacy got so frustrated that she stood up and walked out of the room.

12 Sometimes one's job can become so monotonous and boring that one is left with no option but to call it quits.

13 Since the way we learn is by making mistakes, the greatest risk of all is to wait too long to begin making those mistakes.

Part 2 목적을 나타내는 구 & 문장 (~하기 위하여, ~하도록 하기 위해)

01 She is here **to have** a talk with John.
그녀는 여기 있다　　존과 대화를 하기 위해

02 He talked quietly **in order to avoid** drawing attention to himself.
피하기 위해

03 Jenny went on tiptoe **so as not to disturb** her mother.
방해하지 않기 위해

04 Farmers use pesticides **so that they can bring** higher crop yields.
그들이 가져오도록 하기 위해　　더 높은 곡식 생산량을

05 I left a message to your secretary **in order that you would know** we have come.
네가 알도록 하기 위해　　　우리가 왔었다는

06 **To understand** how human body works, you need some knowledge of chemistry.

07 We should use public transportation **so that we can reduce** the impact on climate change.

08 She did everything **so as to prevent** quarreling among the candidates.

09 It is important to isolate patients with infectious diseases so that others will not become sick.

10 Sunlight is needed in order for the process of *photosynthesis to take place in plants. (광합성)

11 Even though she was not in a good condition, she showed us an excellent performance so that the audience might not get disappointed.

12 He gives his children some money after they do some house chores in order to teach the ultimate goal of an allowance.

CHECK POINT 12

❖ **배운 것 중에서 아는 문장이 나올 때는 기분이 Up!**

01 The value of morality is easy to forget.

02 Grain is easy to make you feel full.

03 She was frustrated to find out that her suggestion was rejected.

04 His efforts to achieve his goal were too precious to ignore.

05 The distance to work is close enough for me to commute.

06 She was so exhausted that she could rarely be aware of his presence.

07 His parents were so disappointed in him that they didn't speak to him all day.

08 It is too important to forget that honesty is a vital element of her success.

09 In severe cases, some students even do something terrible to draw an attention.

10 He decided to abandon the treatment in order to stop a temporary memory loss.

11 He put the wide base to make the structure much more stable.

12 Scientists are studying *meteorites so that they can understand their biological origins. (운석)

13 To perceive what he was trying to say, I fully paid attention to him.

Part 3 분사 구문

* 분사구문은 접속사가 있는 문장을 현재분사 형태로 전환해서 사용하는 형식으로 쓰이는 접속사는 시간, 이유, 조건, 양보의 4가지이며, 그 중에서 **시간과 이유**가 대부분을 차지합니다.

* 분사 구문 만드는 법

  (A) 접속사 생략

  (B) 앞 뒤 주어 같으면 생략

  (C) 동사 시간대가 같으면 동사~ing

01 When (While) he walked (was walking)
Walking home from school, he met someone with a dog. (분사구문은 항상 ~ing로 시작)
그가 학교에서 집으로 걸어가는 동안에(때)

02 As the actress was rich and successful, she turned to charity work.
Being rich and successful, the actress turned to charity work.
부유하고 성공했기 때문에   그 여배우는 자선사업에 눈을 돌렸다.

03 부정어는 문장 앞으로
As I am not able to swim, I feel depressed.
Not being able to swim, I feel depressed.
수영할 수 없어서   나는 우울하다.

04 She had dinner, watching TV. (동시 동작)
그녀는 저녁 식사를 했다, TV를 보면서

He opened the door, stepping inside. (연속 동작)
그는 문을 열었다,   들어가면서 안으로

3-1 시간과 이유 (when, as)

> When she was left to herself, 문장 앞에 being이 나오면 생략 가능해서 과거분사로 시작
> **01** **(Being) Left** to herself, she could finally enjoy meditating.
>   그녀가 혼자 남겨졌을 때   그녀는 마침내 명상하는 것을 즐길 수 있었다.
>
> **02** **As he didn't participate** in the run, 생략을 하면 (not, never)는 문두에
>   **Not participating** in the run, he didn't get a t-shirt.
>   그는 달리기에 참여하지 않아서.   그는 티셔츠를 받지 않았다.

03 **Carrying** a heavy pile of books, he caught his foot on a step.

04 **Storing up** nuts for winter, squirrels are never worried about food.

05 **Bothered** by her husband's snoring, she kicked the poor man.

06 Being an eternal optimist, he always has nothing to worry about.

07 Not wanting to be late for the meeting, he took a cab.

08 While talking on a phone, Mike suddenly hung up on me.

09 Not being able to breathe deeply, I have to get my lung examined.

10 Walking on the red carpet, I felt like a royal appearance.

11 Having a big advantage over my opponents, I can easily beat them.

12 Frightened by its sudden appearance, I yelled "Snake!".

13 When asked a rude question, she was calm and even looked indifferent to it.

14 Estimated to be at least 700 years old, the tree is protected by the villagers.

15 Grown in tropical countries, the pepper was the most valuable spice of all.

16 Noticing that flames poured out of the windows of the building, he managed to escape.

17 Being a highly flammable liquid, it should be handled with much care.

18 Not wanting to hurt his feelings, I avoided the question.

19 Being assigned to work in a Chicago bank, I had to find another place to stay.

20 Appointed as chairman, he felt not only a huge burden but also felt grateful for their support.

21 Armed with scientific knowledge, people build tools and machines that transform the way we live, making our lives much easier and better.

3-2 분사 구문 (if, though)

>   If you rotate
> **01** **Rotating** a door knob to the left,   you can open the door.
>   만약 당신이 문손잡이를 왼쪽으로 돌리면,
>
>   Though his company was founded,
> **02** **Founded** last year,   his company made a huge profit.
>   비록 작년에 설립되었을지라도

03 **Having to proceed** with extreme caution, we will take a one step at a time.

05 **Noticing her new hair style**, he said nothing about it.

04 **Reaching an agreement**, the firm will compensate workers for their loss of income.

06 **Applied correctly**, the paint will never peel.

07 **Looked after carefully**, these boots will last for many years.

3-3 예외도 있어요 (주어가 다른 경우, 시간대가 다른 경우)

* 앞 뒤 시간대가 다르면 먼저 발생한 일을 완료형으로

> As I had been unemployed (더 먼저 발생한 일을 과거완료로 나타냄)
> **01 Having been unemployed** for over two years, I found it difficult to get work.
>   2년 넘게 실직 상태여서   나는 일을 구하기가 어렵다는 것을 알았다.

02 Having prepared everything for the party, she felt relieved.

03 Having taken the wrong train, I found myself in New York, not in New Work.

04 Having lived through difficult times together, they were very close friends.

05 Not having been properly compensated for the damage, residents in the area are furious at the decision.

* 앞 뒤 주어가 다르면 생략 불가

> As the task was done quickly (앞 뒤 주어 다른 경우 생략 불가)
> **01 The task done quickly,** we could call it a day.
>   업무가 일찍 끝나서,   우리는 일찍 끝낼 수 있었다.

02 Nobody having any more questions to ask, **the meeting** came to a close.

03 His hands trembling, **he** looked out at the audience. (tremble: 떨다)

04 There being no other way, we had no choice but to accept their offer.

05 It being a rainy day, a thanksgiving ceremony was held inside the building.

Exercise 5

▶ 다음 중 옳은 것을 고르시오.

01 (Having not, Not having) enough time, we couldn't go to a movie.

02 (Surprised, Surprising) at the news, she was speechless.

03 (To walk, Walking, Walked) along the street, I met my old friend.

04 (Changed, Changing) your habits, you will be successful.

05 Badly (injuring, injured) in the accident, he couldn't walk.

06 (Lost, Losing) all his money, he had nowhere to go.

07 (Not doing, Doing not) any exercise, he never gets healthy.

08 (Disappointing, Disappointed) with her attitude, she gave him up.

09 (Understanding, Understand) what he was trying to say, I nodded.

10 (Found, Finding) in the deep sea, it still looks new.

3-4 동시동작, 연속동작

* 동시 동작인 경우에 주절의 문장이 끝나고 다음 문장이 ~ing로 시작하면 ~하면서라고 해석한다.
연속 동작은 한 행동이 끝나고 바로 다른 행동으로 이어지는 것을 의미한다.

1. as 혹은 while의 접속사 생략   2. 연속동작 (and)   3. with (~인 채로, ~하면서, 때문에)

01 She looked into a mirror, **rubbing** her hair with a towel. (동시동작)
　　　　　　　　　　　　　　as or while she was rubbing
그녀는 거울을 바라보았다　　문지르면서 그녀의 머리를 수건으로

02 His reckless driving ended, **resulting** in the death of two passengers. (연속동작)
　　　　　　　　　　　　　　and resulted
그는 무모한 운전은 끝이 났다,　결과를 낳으면서 두 명의 승객의 사망으로

03 He was sitting on his chair **with** his arms crossed.
그는 그의 의자에 앉아있었다.　그의 팔짱을 낀 채로

04 The two men are standing side by side, **breathing** hard on heated asphalt road.

05 Thousands of people crossed the border, **seeking** refuge camp from the war.

06 He encouraged hatred toward each other, eventually **causing** more racism.

07 Running to catch a bus, she tripped and sprained her ankle.

08 A snow storm covered the roadway, trapping dozens of drivers in their cars.

09 Pollution and fossil fuels give us global warming, resulting in extreme weather.

10 The manager led the way through the office, explaining the process in easy terms.

11 Using their strong flippers, dolphins can go up to the shore and eat as many fish as they want.

12 A praying mantis stands with its front legs folded up high in front of its body.

13 With a frog popping out of the box, we were surprised.

14 With temperatures rising rapidly, people seem to enjoy outside activities.

15 Do you think you can walk with this ball on your head?

16 With David's presentation satisfactory, we gave him a big round of applause.

17 He found a man rolling on the ground with his clothes catching fire.

18 People jump from airplanes with surfboards attached to their feet.

19 She got dressed in white clothes with a red handkerchief carefully tied at her neck.

20 Many people say "I can't do it.", or "I am always like that.", making self-defeating statements.

21 Often the adults behave aggressively themselves, sending children the message that winning is everything.

22 Talk naturally at a pace to suit your listeners, using pauses and silences as well as changing the tone and pitch of your voice to emphasize what you say.

23 When winners make mistakes and get knocked down, however, they quickly get up and try again, firmly believing success is not far.

3-5 그냥 혼자 사용하는 분사 표현 (독립 분사 구문)

- Generally speaking : 일반적으로 말해서
- Strictly speaking : 엄격하게 말해서
- Frankly speaking : 솔직하게 말해서
- Judging from : ~로 판단해 보건대
- Providing that : 만약 ~라면
- Considering that : ~고려해 볼 때
- Compared A with B: 비교해 볼 때
- Simply put : 간단히 말해서
- Granting (granted) that : 가령 ~한다 하더라도

01 Judging from my experience, positive people do things better.

02 Simply put, you were right about the choice you made.

03 Compared to our small place, Jake's house seemed like a palace.

04 Strictly speaking, spiders are not insects, although most people think they are.

05 You can borrow my car, providing I can have it back by six o'clock.

06 If you use straw as bedding for farm animals, generally speaking, you will improve the welfare of those animals.

❖ 배경 지식은 독해를 통해서

01 Working out regularly, he can stay in shape.

02 Sitting on a bench, we could see a ship on the horizon.

03 Not being selected as the singer of the year, she felt disappointed.

04 Not having recognized the symptoms, the doctor told him to go to the general hospital.

05 Holding the hair-dryer in her left hand, Susie cut her hair.

06 We see lots of victims every day, worldwide, resulting from the lack of education.

07 Jenny wrote a paper saying vitamin C prevents colds, using her data as evidence.

08 Considering current circumstance we are under, we need an alternative way to solve the problem.

09 There being no other way, we had no choice but to take his offer.

10 The captain looked out the window with his pipe in his mouth.

11 We are very wasteful of natural resources, thinking that there will be enough land, air, water forever.

12 Considering products with material properties, such as clothes, consumers like goods they can touch in stores.

13 Surprisingly, about 40% of the people of Argentina are originally from Italy, compared to 30% who come from Spain.

딱!
한권으로 정리되는
구문독해

Chapter 4
접속사

Part 1. **등위접속사와 병렬구조**

Part 2. **상관접속사**

Part 3. **시간, 조건의 부사절**

Part 4. **비록 ~일지라도(양보절) 그리고 구**

Part 5. **복합 관계부사**

Part 6. **접속사 as**

Part 7. **내가 모를 수도 있는 접속사**

Part 1 등위 접속사와 병렬구조 (1)

* 문법적으로 같은 것들을 연결시켜 주는 접속사: 명사와 명사, 형용사와 형용사 혹은 같은 동사 형태끼리 (and, or, but, for, so)

* 문장에서 단어나 구, 절 등이 연속적으로 나열 되거나, 등위접속사(**and, or** 등) 또는 상관접속사 (both A and B, either A or B 등)에 의해 연결될 때 연결 대상의 구조 및 성격을 일치시켜야 한다.

01 He eats just **vegetables** and **fruits** for dinner. (단어+단어 = 와, 과로 해석)

02 You can **go** up to the shore and **eat** as many fish as you want. (동사+동사 = 그리고 로 해석)
[병렬구조: go and eat]

03 The researchers also found that 88% of smokers **were** bald or **had** gray hair.

04 Pavarotti **was born** with a wonderful voice, but he always **took** singing lessons.

05 I **appreciate** all the effort you've put in teaching **and wish** you a happy retirement.

06 He is really good at playing basketball, but not at swimming.

07 Walking is a good way to stay healthy, save energy, and enjoy fresh air.

08 A language is best learned by making mistakes and correcting them.

09 You should remember to wash your hands after touching animals or spending time in areas where animals are housed or exhibited.

10 Children who type for a long time or use a computer mouse too much can develop problems to their bodies.

1-2 등위 접속사 (and, but, so, for, yet)

01 He doesn't want to buy any chemical medicines, **for** they are expensive and unhealthy.
그는 어떤 화학 약품도 사고 싶어 하지 않는다. 왜냐하면 그것들은 비싸고 건강에 좋지 않기 때문이다.
왜냐하면 (주로 앞에 ,가 나옴)

02 John plays soccer well, **yet** his favorite sport is basketball.
존은 축구를 잘한다, 그렇지만 그가 가장 좋아하는 스포츠는 농구이다.
그러나 (그럼에도 불구하고)

03 She didn't speak to anyone **and** nobody spoke to her.

04 She has a job interview, **so** she will go to London next week.

05 He puts on weight easily, **for** he always eats fast food and he eats everything very quickly.

06 She says nice words to us, yet we shouldn't trust her.

07 Mike is really tall, so he has an advantage playing basketball.

08 Kevin was a convicted criminal, yet many people admired him.

09 He found it increasingly difficult to read, for his eyesight was beginning to fail.

10 She had previous experience, so she seemed the best candidate.

11 The purpose of the scheme is not to help the employers but to provide work for young people.

12 Every three seconds, someone needs blood. Yet less than five percent of the population donates blood.

Part 2 상관 접속사

2-1. 상관접속사:

접속사가 두 개의 연결고리가 되어 A와 B (단어 혹은 구)를 연결하는 역할을 한다.

a) not only A but (also) B   b) B as well as A   c) not A but B

01 This car is **not only economical but** it **also** feels good to drive.
  이 차는   경제적일뿐만 아니라   또한 운전하기에 기분이 좋다.
  (A뿐만 아니라 / B 또한)

= This car feels good to drive **as well as** is economical. (마찬가지로)

02 The most important thing in this game is **not to win but take part in**. (A가 아니라 B)
  이기는 것이 아니라 참여하는 것이다.

03 Not only **will she paint** the wall but also the fence. (도치 문장)

04 Not only Mike but also **John seems** to have gotten used to driving in Seoul. (B에 따라 수의 일치)

05 Please don't approach the customer **eagerly**, but **cautiously**.

06 It was the right thing to do **as well as** good, sensible politics.

07 Not only **do the nurses want** a pay increase, but also they want reduced hours. (도치)

08 I not only admire his works but also respect his way of thinking.

09 This exercise will strengthen not only your stomach muscles but also your lung function.

10 Reinforce the security around the building as well as the gate.

11 Not only their family problems, but also their financial problems interfered with my work.

2-2 상관접속사

(A) either A or B **(B)** neither A nor B **(C)** both A and B

01 I will **eat either carrots or peas** for dinner. (A 혹은 B 중에 하나)
나는 먹을 것이다   당근이나 콩을   저녁으로

02 He has **neither talent nor desire** to learn. (A도 아니고 B도 아닌)
그는 재능도 없고   배우려고 하는 욕구도 없다.

03 Your work is **both neat and accurate**. (A와 B 둘 다)
너의 작업은   깔끔하면서 정확하다.

04 **Either the lion or the cheetah was** not able to capture its prey. (B의 수일치)

05 Their bodies regulate temperature properly **neither in summer** nor **in winter**.

06 **Both** salt **and** sugar were used to preserve food.

07 He showed neither gratitude nor complaint for the service provided.

08 Both of the candidates didn't feel annoyed by my private questions.

09 This structure is neither remarkable nor essential for people working here.

10 Either you or your partner should try to cultivate your power to control the employees.

11 As Isaac Newton grew older, he was either absorbed in thought or engaged in some books of mathematics or natural science.

❖ 배운 것을 해석으로 확인!!!

01 It is an unnecessary and excessive punishment to deprive prisoners of their right to vote.

02 The Sun is a very important part of our life, yet we know so little about it.

03 I can't recogize what she looks like, for I haven't seen her for a long time.

04 Set your sights on reaching a level of achievement that is both satisfying and sustainable.

05 This system enables the vehicle to use either natural gas or a conventional fuel.

06 One-sided relationships usually don't work, and neither do one-sided conversations.

07 Both cats and dogs have a much narrower frequency range than bats which have the second widest frequency range.

08 If someone spills drink on the carpet at a party, one not only apologizes for it, but also offers to clear it up.

09 The true source of liver damage might be either years of drinking or eating foods that are high in fat or processed.

10 Prisoners are shut away not only to protect the society, but also to symbolize society's disgust at their acts.

11 The most dangerous threat to our ability to concentrate is not that we use our smartphone during working hours, but that we use it too irregularly.

Part 3 시간과 조건의 부사절

* 시간대가 미래를 가리킨다 할지라도 현재형을 사용

A when: ~일 때
B while: ~하는 동안에
C as soon as: ~하자마자(the moment)
D until: ~일 때 까지
E once: 일단 ~하면

A if: 만약 ~라면
B as long as: ~하는 한
C unless: ~하지 않는 한
D in case: ~하는 경우에
E every time: ~할 때 마다 (each time, whenever)

미래 대신 현재 동사 사용

01 **When** you **have** a talk with the two candidates, you will find some relative merits.
당신이 대화를 할 때

02 **If** they **threaten** to take you to the court, please contact your lawyer right away.
만약 그들이 위협한다면 데려간다고 당신을 법원으로,

03 She maintained a high status in the community **until** she lost her reputation.

04 **As soon as** she realized she had done something wrong, she apologized to the man.

05 **Once** you finish drawing the family portrait, he will hang it on the wall.

06 All the cars are tested for defects **before** they leave the factory.

07 The tension was becoming unbearable **after** he brought up the subject.

08 **As long as** you combine a theory with practice, people will start investing.

09 **If** you are a woman, there are still many obstacles to overcome to gain equality.

10 **Unless** you are in conflicts with your parents, it is good for you to stay with them.

11 **In case** the building burns down, we'll get the insurance money.

Part 4 비록 ~일지라도 (양보 절) 그리고 구

* (Even) though, although: 비록 ~일지라도 (S+V) / even if: 설사~라 할지라도
despite, in spite of: ~에도 불구하고 (전치사이므로 다음에 명사 혹은 동명사만 나옴)

01 **Though she resigned** her position, her power is still intensively influential.
비록 그녀가 그녀의 지위를 사임했을지라도,   그녀의 힘은 여전히 엄청난 영향력이 있다.

02 **Even if** she says "Yes",   it doesn't necessarily mean "Yes".
설사 그녀가 네라고 말한다 할지라도, 그것이 반드시 네를 의미하는 것은 아니다.

03 **Despite** my limited success, I could bring a lot of profit.
나의 제한된 성공에도 불구하고   나는 큰 이익을 가져올 수 있었다.

04 **Although** she suffered from terminal disease, she never thought of going to hospital.

05 **Even though** he had a good intention, the way he helped her was wrong.

06 **In spite of** being a free country, it seems to be under domination of America.

07 Although her best friend is one of the employees, she is rarely seen talking with her.

08 Though we consume this product, we are not 100% satisfied with its quality.

09 Despite the fact that the economy has gone into recession, our company is surviving.

10 Even if a family can't eat together every night, they should try to get together at least once a week.

11 Despite the fact that the disease is so prevalent, treatment is still far from satisfactory.

12 Despite the challenges she faced in being the only woman in medical school, she didn't give up and eventually gained the respect of her professors and peers.

Part 5 복합 관계부사 와 그 외 식구들: 접속사 역할을 하는 복합 관계부사
(~이던지 간에)

*whatever, whoever, wherever, however (no matter 의문사): ~일지라도
whether A or B: 이던지 간에,　while (whereas): ~ 인 반면에

01 **Whatever** creature it is, it has its ancestor.
　　　그것이 어떤 생물이든이 간에,　그것은 조상을 가지고 있습니다.

02 **Wherever** he may go, he is sure to make friends.
　　　그는 어디를 가든지 간에　　그는 친구를 사귈 것이 확실하다.

03 **No matter** how old we may get, in our minds, we will always be 14.
　　　아무리 우리가 나이가 들지라도

04 **While** she knows everything about flowers, she is not an expert in doing her own business.

05 **Whether** you agree to her plan or not, she will proceed with it.

06 A young person learns his dreams, **whereas** an adult never pursues his dreams.

07 However carefully you have planned, there might be something you never expected.

08 No matter where your destination is, you should take a first step toward it.

09 Some children like academic subjects while others prefer to make things with their hands.

10 While fantasy involves imagining an idealized future, expectation is actually based on a person's past experiences.

11 Nature takes millions of years to create new organisms, whereas scientists can create them in just a few days.

12 No matter how a desert is defined, it is a region that can support little plant life because of insufficient moisture and dry soil.

Part 6 접속사 as

* [전치사: as + 명사: ~로서]
　[접속사: as + 주어+동사: ~때, ~ 때문에, ~대로, ~함에 따라, ~에도 불구하고]

01 As I was watching football on TV, the electricity went off.
　　　내가 TV에서 축구를 보려고 했을 때,　　　　　전기가 나갔다.

02 As I know the way, I will tell you how to get there.
　　　내가 길을 알기 때문에,　　내가 어떻게 그곳에 가는지 너에게 말해 주마.

03 As she mentioned, another accident occurred again.
　　　그녀가 언급했던 대로,　　　　다른 사고가 또 발생했다.

04 As the weather is getting warmer, people begin to enjoy outdoor activities. (때와 같은 의미로 사용)
　　　날씨가 따뜻해짐에 따라,　　　　　사람들이 야외 활동을 즐기기 시작한다.

05 As popular as he is, he makes a small income. (앞에 as가 생략되는 경우도 있음)
　　　그는 인기가 있을지라도,　　　그는 수입이 적다.

06 Leave the bag **as it is**. *** (학생들이 가장 해석을 못하는 부분)

07 Do **as** I say, otherwise you will get punished.

08 Most of the characters can be pronounced **as** they are written.

09 "Thank you," he replied as he blew out one of the two candles on the table.

10 As he knocked on the door, a giant man came out of the house.

11 As I stated before, we have to assign a person with a new duty to do the work.

12 As I didn't submit my report on time, I will probably get terrible grades.

13 The octopus can change its color in seconds as it moves across different backgrounds.

Part 7 내가 모를 수도 있는 접속사

01 Since the mood of the meeting was distinctly pessimistic, the boss kept silent. (~ 때문에)
회의의 분위기가 뚜렷하게 비관이라서   보스는 침묵을 지켰다.

02 While she is a likable girl, she can be extremely difficult to work with. (~인 반면에)
그녀는 호감이 가는 소녀인 반면에,   그녀는 함께 일하기가 매우 어려울 수 있다.

03 Social status influenced the fashion of footwear **just as** it impacted the arts and architecture.
사회적 신분이 신발의 유행에 영향을 미쳤다   (꼭 ~ 처럼) 꼭 그것이 예술과 건축에 영향을 미쳤던 것처럼

04 Now that we're all here, let's start the meeting. (~이니까)
우리 모두가 여기 있으니까,   회의를 시작합시다.

05 I've been lucky **in that** I have never had to worry about money. (~라는 점에서)
나는 운이 좋았다   내가 돈에 대해서 걱정하지 않아도 된다는 점에서

06 Once I get him a job, he'll be fine. (일단 ~하면)
내가 일단 그에게 직업을 구해주면, 그는 괜찮을 것이다.

07 Given that the circumstances, you've done really well.
상황을 고려한다면,   너는 정말로 잘했다.

08 The Sun is a very important part of our life, **yet** we know so little about it. (그러나)

09 I regretted what I had said **in that** it made you angry.

10 Now that I think of what you have done, I acted the same way when I was your age.

11 Since they were not emotionally mature enough, they always had a fight and ended up divorcing.

12 Now that you're older, you're probably more self-conscious about letting people see your tears.

13 By the time a child is five, he will have watched hundreds of hours of television. (~일 때쯤)

14 Once you receive your new passport, your old passport is not valid for international travel.

CHECK POINT 15

❖ **반복 연습도 중요해요!!!**

01 As soon as we are born, the world gets to work on us and transforms us into social units.

02 A lie can travel halfway around the world while the truth is still putting on its shoes. [Mark Twain]

03 You must not dive unless you have been properly trained.

04 Once things become really tough, it'll be hard to stay motivated.

05 If this position requires a man of high moral standards, he is not the right man.

06 Nothing ever grew boring no matter how often they were repeated.

07 I will accept your decision, no matter which choice you make.

08 Poverty is a direct consequence of overpopulation no matter what excuse there may be.

09 Whoever may pull out this sword from the stone, we all will regard him as a leader.

10 Now that we know each other a little better, we will get along fine.

11 The new system is similar to the old one in that there is still a strong central government.

12 As I explained on the phone, your request will be considered at the next meeting.

13 Since I got a distinction in all the subjects in my High School examination, I am happy.

14 Dilemma tales are like folk tales in that they are usually short, simple, and driven entirely by plot.

15 The Universe is one organic whole, no matter how diverse and wide it may seem to be.

16 Now that I have paid all my debts, a load is off my mind.

17 No matter how expensive environmentally friendly product is, it is worth buying.

18 No matter how vague the symptoms, you need to be careful in early pregnancy.

19 Remember that you won't be able to cancel the contract once you've signed.

20 While there was no conclusive evidence, most people thought he was guilty.

21 Since we live in such an achievement-driven world, it's very easy to fall into the habit of focusing on what's lacking in your life.

22 While it is seemingly unproductive, avoidance may actually be useful if the situation is short-term or of minor importance.

23 Domestic violence happens when one person uses force upon another person they have or had a relationship with.

24 Even though sharks' jaws and teeth make them fierce, it's their sense of hearing that truly makes them great hunters.

25 Given that the patients have some disabilities, we still try to enable them to be as independent as possible.

딱!
한권으로 정리되는
구문독해

Chapter 5
명사절

Part 1. **명사절**

Part 2. **if, whether**

Part 3. **명사 역할 의문사**

Part 4. **what (것)**

Part 5. **복합관계 대명사**

Part 1 명사절 (명사가 나오는 자리에 주어+동사가 나오며 접속사는 that, if, whether)

01 **That she was an eye-witness of the murder case** is not clear. (주어)
그녀가 살인사건의 목격자였다는 것이 　　　　　　　　　 명확하지 않다.

It is not clear **that** she was an eye-witness of the murder case.
가주어　　　　진주어

02 **The fact** is **that I really admire** his ability to stay calm in stressful situations. (보어)
사실은　　　내가 정말로 감탄한다는 것이다 그의 능력을 / 침착하게 있는 스트레스 상황에서

03 **We** all **know** **that we live** in an era of instant communication. (목적어)
우리 모두는 안다　　　우리가 살고 있는 것을 [살고 있다고] 즉각적인 의사소통의 시대에

04 At first I got **the impression** = **that he wasn't interested in this plan**. (동격)
처음에 나는 받았다　인상을　　　　그가 이 계획에 관심이 없다는 (해석 가능)

05 **It** is certain **that** my grandfather's inheritance has enabled us to buy our first house.

06 It occurred to her **that** if she didn't try to compete in the tryout, her dream would never come true.

07 The fact is **that** no one gives us a specific reason why we have to wait.

08 The best advantage of a package holiday is that it's simple to organize.

09 You must realize **that** buying bottled water is nothing more than a waste of money.

10 A strange thing about the Sun is that most of it is not solid, but it is made up of mostly gas.

11 Do you know that the search for an actor to play Harry potter took almost a year?

12 Remember that the learning style that works for your friend won't necessarily work for you.

13 Many say that following trends is stupid and that they feel no pressure whatsoever.

14 Scientists have found that the way the brain works is far more complicated than they had thought.

15 This insect has a red coloring that warns predators that it is toxic.

16 The opinion that the death penalty should be abolished will get stronger and stronger.

17 Do you have any evidence that I cheated on the test?

18 Another thing to consider is that the real-name system will make people posting messages act more carefully.

19 The UN released a report that we have developed so successfully that we have more food per person than at any previous time in human history.

20 The easiest way to know that lightning can really strike the same spot many times is to look at buildings that aren't damaged when they're struck by lightning.

Part 2 if, whether

* 주로 주절에 동사가 의구심을 나타내는 의미를 갖는 경우에 ~인지의 의미를 갖는 if는 만약의 의미를 갖는 if와 혼동을 피하기 위해 맨 앞에 나올 수는 없고, whether는 위치에 구애를 받지 않으며 or not이 항상 나오는 것은 아니다.

01 Check **if** the nail is secure and hang your picture on it.
확인해라 못이 안전한지   그리고 걸어라 너의 그림을 그것 위에

02 **Whether** a book is a "great gift" **or not depends** on **whether** we can read it in a creative way.
책이 훌륭한 책인지 아닌지는   달려있다   우리가 그것을 읽는지 창의적인 방법으로

03 She might ask you **if** you like her new look and you may think it is not at all attractive.

04 I wonder **if** Mike will apply for a job at the company where you work.

05 He will find out **if** the memo should be distributed to everyone in the office before 3:00.

06 In our increasingly fast-paced world, you tend to think you can tell if you like someone immediately.

07 At night, Newtown used to look up to the stars, wondering whether they were worlds like our own.

08 No one can confirm whether or not she actually boarded the flight.

09 Whether you have a ticket or not, please proceed to gate 33 where your plane is now boarding.

10 Mike should be here to see if the ring she showed us was genuine diamond.

***11** Whether or not you'd like to believe your ears, the company has launched the new drug. (~ 이던지 간에)

***12** Whether you're a boy a girl, you may think crying isn't mature.

Part 3 명사 역할 의문사

> **01** One important influence can be **whom** you select as friends.
> 한가지 중요한 영향은   당신이 누구를 친구로 선택하느냐가 될 수 있다.
>
> **02** The book is about **where** the dinosaurs laid their eggs.
> 그 책은 공룡이 그들의 알을 어디에 낳았느냐에 관한 것이다.

03 Genes determine **how** your personalities are formed.

04 **Who** gets the credit for a good idea should not be important.

05 In a job interview, ask not **what** your employer can do for you, but what you can do for your employer.

06 I don't know where I can find a patriotic person like you.

07 It is not what you have but what you are that matters.

08 I was convinced of her honesty by proving what type of person she was.

09 First, you have to find out what is like living in New York city.

10 I remember how she always used to have fresh flowers in the house.

11 No one knows what it feels like to be in such a terrible situation.

12 Which is the best way is not important as far as I am concerned.

13 Friendship isn't about whom you have known the longest, but is about who came and never left you side.

Part 4   What (것)

*what은 [것]의 의미를 갖으며 **자체가 명사라 앞에 명사가 나올 수 없고**, 뒤에 나오는 문장이 해석이 안 된다.

01   **What** she did / **made** him upset. (주어)
　　　　그녀가 했던 것이　　만들었다 그를 화나게

02   Passion is **what** every one of teachers should have when they teach. (보어)
　　　　열정은　　　　　선생님들의 모두가 가져야 하는 것이다　　　　　　그들이 가르칠 때

03   We are going to replace **what** we have with this new equipment. (목적어)
　　　　우리는　　대체할 것이다　　　우리가 가지고 있는 것을　　　이 새로운 장비로

04   **What we will confront** is fierce competition between the companies.

05   Money is **what gives it its value**.

06   We didn't address **what our boss had mentioned** during the meeting.

07   There are no limitations in what you can do except the limitations in your mind.

08   Use what you know about yourself to find the most effective way to study.

09   What she studies at college is natural phenomena such as earthquakes and typhoons.

10   What made Mike fire Jenny was that the racial remarks she made during the meeting.

11   She spent a lot of water from the tank, and there is only one-fifth of what it was.

12   Contrary to what many people believe, bats are not likely to attack humans.

13   It is what is inside that matters.

14 You have what it takes to be our leader.

15 Don't tell the persons interviewing you what's on your resume.

16 What most children have is a keen interest in how the country is changing.

17 What I thought was right proved to be wrong in the end.

18 Researchers say that what tastes good or bad can depend on the taster's genes.

19 The peasant farmers had to pay rent or give the owner half of what they grew.

20 We should be able to see what is potentially good in people, regardless of our first impressions.

21 All human beings think that what they have to say is worth hearing.

22 Awareness of what one does not know can be a good way to acquire knowledge.

23 Most people like to see in pictures what they would also like to see in reality.

24 The value of what you have to sell does not necessarily increase when the market expands, and it may decrease.

25 In the contemporary society, we are all too often judged by what we own rather than by what we are.

26 Being grateful means thinking more about what you have and what's right than about what's wrong, what's missing, and what you don't have.

Part 5 복합관계 대명사 whoever, whomever, whatever, whichever

* 명사 역할 whoever (anyone that: ~하는 사람은 누구든지) whatever (anything that: 무엇이든지)

01 **Whoever** makes a threat against you **will be arrested**. (주어)
당신을 위협하는 사람은 누구든지 체포될 것이다.

02 Do **whatever** it takes to do to make you happy. (목적어)
해라 무엇이던지   할 필요가 있는   너를 행복하게 하기 위해

03 Nowadays, **whatever** celebrities do becomes fashionable.

04 He will hire **whoever** is most qualified among the applicants.

05 **Whichever** player scores the highest number of points will be the winner.

06 Give this award to **whomever** you think deserves it.

07 Tom's teacher wished him the best of luck in whatever he chose to do after leaving school.

08 Whoever we appoint for this position will be dealing directly with our clients.

09 Please ask permission from whoever pays the phone bill before making your call.

10 Whatever you're going through has nothing to do with what I am doing now.

11 Whatever you do, please do not harm others. (복합 관계부사: 비교)

❖ 해석은 되는데 도대체 무슨 말이지?

01 Whether or not we go to Spain for our holiday depends on the cost.

02 What sculpture is to a block of marble, education is to the soul. (A is to B = C is to D)

03 What enabled me to accept his offer was the advantages I could get.

04 The problem is that life is sometimes unfair and we can be victimized.

05 Those who have the taste for ancient architecture can see what our tremendous museum offers.

06 It is certain that we will have to rely more on alternate energy sources.

07 I'm not sure if we can increase our efficiency though we really examine how we are doing things.

08 Don't deny the fact we all are under pressure to look good, sometimes look better than others.

09 The way she told me about the recipe is not like what you just mentioned.

10 I'll pay whatever you feel is a fair price.

11 Whoever wins the election is going to have a tough job getting the economy back on its feet.

12 A recent survey revealed that eight out of ten adults over the age of 35 expressed dissatisfaction at the lack of personal space in their lives.

❖ 배웠는데 자꾸 잊어버리는 구절

01 This kind of accident **used to occur** in the area of the city. [발생하곤 했다]

02 The bulldozer would **be used to load** heavy equipment. [싣는데 사용 된다]

03 It takes some time to **get used to new glasses**, just like anything else at first. [새 안경에 익숙해지다]

04 You will **get(be) used to driving** in busy traffic after a while. [운전하는 것에 익숙해지다]

05 The police **couldn't help abandoning** their search after looking for the lost child for over a year.

06 We **can't help but put** top priority on your safety. [놓지 않을 수 없다]

07 You **can't be too** careful **when it comes to taking** financial advice. [~에 관해]

08 We have to **keep (prevent)** this pest **from spreading** to our field. [막다 ~ 확산되는 것을]

09 She and I just **happened to have** the same name. We are not related at all. [우연히 갖게 되다]

10 The animals in the desert have **managed to adapt** themselves to its conditions. ~하게 되다 [그럭저럭]

11 John **doesn't mean to**, but sometimes his blunt manner makes it look like he's rude or rough.

12 I **forgot to distribute** this memo to everyone in the office before 3:00. [할 것을 잊다]

13 Inertia is the tendency of an object to remain still **unless** a force is **applied to** it.

14 Some will resign from big business and **devote themselves to turning** an idea or hobby into a business of their own. [= dedicate]

Chapter 6
관계대명사

Part 1. **관계대명사 (주격, 목적격)**

Part 2. **관계사 생략**

Part 3. **전치사 + 관계사**

Part 4. **소유격 whose**

Part 5. **계속적**

Part 6. **수를 나타내는 of 관계대명사**

Part 7. **관계사에 삽입 절이 들어 있는 경우**

Part 8. **관계부사**

Part 1 관계대명사 (주격, 목적격)

*두 문장에서 공통되는 대명사를 생략하면서 두 문장을 하나로 연결하는 기능을 하며
관계사 다음에 나오는 문장이 앞에 명사를 꾸며 주어 이것을 형용사 절이라고 한다.

A. 주격: who, which, that은 뒤에 동사나, 주어+동사가 나와도 되는, 즉 주격, 목적격 사용이 다 가능하다.

01 I decided not to hire **the man** who **demanded** more pay.
요구했던

02 **The man** who **damaged** my car **ran away**.
피해를 입힌

03 The plants usually grow on **dark rocks** which **hold heat from the sun**.
어두운 바위에서 가두는 열을 태양으로부터

04 **The refugees** who **come across** the border in vast numbers **have** no where to go.
난민들은 넘어오는 갈 곳이 없다.

05 I admire the man who **places** a high moral value on the family unit.

06 We did not fully grasp the significance of the events that **frightened** the residents.

07 Knowledge has value only in the hands of someone who **has** the ability to think well.

08 Life on earth probably began with simple chemical reactions which occurred naturally.

09 There were a series of experiments about factors which affect the way of people's behaviors.

10 **Those** who can't find time during the day can get their exercise at 24/7 fitness center. 중요:(사람들: 일반)

11 In offices, workers who have windows near their desks work harder than those who don't.

12 Children who do badly in school tests often perceive themselves to be failures.

13 Going to bed late may reduce the likelihood of seeing morning light which resets the body clock.

14 Before the Civil War, the economy of the South depended upon the plantation system which made use of slave labor.

15 There was a blind man who could see well enough to describe things in detail only by holding his hand over objects.

16 Scientists who have observed plants growing in the dark have found that they are vastly different in appearance, form, and function from those grown in the light.

17 People who are genetically similar may be less able to deal with unexpected changes, such as the outbreak of a new disease.

Exercise 6

▶ 다음 중 옳은 것을 고르시오.

01 The boy who does exercise every day with his friends (look / looks) healthy.

02 The man who sent me the flowers (work / works) at a bank.

03 The museum which holds many interesting paintings (open / opens) at 10 in the morning.

04 The girl who comes here and cleans the street up never (want / wants) any money.

05 The boys who are singing on the stage (is / are) the same classmates.

06 The volunteer who helps us usually (comes / come) here on Sunday.

B. 목적격 관계대명사
*who, whom 둘 다 사용가능하며, which, that도 주격, 목적격에 사용

01 She likes **the souvenir** which **he bought** at your shop. (it 대신에 which)
　　　명사　　　　　　　그가 샀던

　　　　　　　　　　　　　　　　　　　단수동사 (주어가 너무 멀리 있는 경우 동사 확인)
02 **The number of experts** that **he mentioned at the meeting** is no more than three.
　　　전문가들의 수　　　　　그가 회의에서 언급한　　　　　3명에 불과하다.

03 I spent two hours talking to a person who[m] **I'd met** only once before. (who도 whom도 가능)

04 Drought and flood are disasters that **we undergo** every year.

05 The career which I pursued suits my real self.

06 I will try to maintain reasonable weight which my doctor suggested.

07 There are some kinds of questions that scientific approach cannot solve.

08 Critical reading is an acquired skill that you will develop with some knowledge and experience.

09 The way which she suggested to solve the problem is rational and reasonable.

10 The book which she has read is important for her literature review.

11 The results that I obtained may invoke positive social change for the citizens.

12 In our lives, we all encounter stress and difficulties which we must overcome.

13 Cartoon characters are used on the backpacks that he has designed for a famous luggage company.

Exercise 7

▶ 옳은 것 고르기

01 She knows the man (who, whom) Maris likes to meet.

02 Mike often rides the bike (that, which) his father bought him on his birthday.

03 This is the lady (who, whom) gave us a big tip.

04 We will meet the students (who, whom) we will take to London next week.

05 They found a girl and a cat (which, that) were sitting on a tree.

06 Tom enjoys talking with the girl (who, whom) Susie introduced to him.

07 The boy who Jenny drove to New York city (like, likes) movies a lot.

08 The bus which goes to the museum (come, comes) here every hour.

09 She told me about the house in (which, that) he lived with his parents.

10 Did you find the ring which John had hidden (it, X)?

11 The man whom Mike pushed hard (look, looks) really upset.

12 The doctors who Mike works with (visit, visits) us once a year.

13 Tom wants to know the name of the song to (which, that) he just listened.

14 Sam will play the music which the stranger (playing, was playing).

15 Jack drives the car which everyone wants to have (it, X).

Part 2 관계사 생략

*관계사 다음에 **주어 + 동사**가 나오면 생략 가능하며, 관계사 다음에 be동사가 나오면 **관계사와 같이 생략할 수 있고**, 관계사 앞에 전치사가 나오면 **생략이 불가능**하다.

01 The illness (**that or which**) he suffered from robbed him of a normal childhood.
그가 겪는 질병은 그에게서 앗아갔다 정상적인 어린 시절을

생략 가능
02 The man **who was** injured in a car accident is in an intensive care room now.
교통사고로 부상당한 그 남자는 지금 중환자실에 있다.

03 You will encounter a few serious problems (**which**) you never expect.

04 One of my most distinct characteristics **is** the diversity of experiences I possess.

05 We can't pass on the corrupt society we live in now to our future generations.

06 Police are trying to trace a young woman I saw near the crime scene.

07 The man infected with Covid 19 a few days ago was found dead in a street.

08 He shot the squirrels digging in his garden to find their nuts.

09 Most children abused by their parents tend to be violent.

10 Most of the people involved in the incident have either died or been severely injured.

11 Our society has changed in ways the founders of social welfare policy couldn't foresee.

12 Water composed of hydrogen and oxygen is vital to all living creatures.

13 All the things we buy just sitting gathering dust are waste.

Part 3 전치사 + 관계사 (전치사 + who or that X)

*관계사 앞에 전치사가 나오면 **관계사를 생략할 수 없고**, who와 that 앞에는 전치사를 쓸 수 없다.

01 The company **for which** I work will be sending me to Europe for business reasons.
　　　내가 일하는 회사는　　　　　　　　나를 보낼 것이다 / 유럽으로 출장 이유로

The company **I work for** will be sending me to Europe for business reasons. (생략 후 전치사 위치 확인)

02 Do you know someone **with whom** I can talk about global warming?
　　　사람을 알고 있나요?　　　　　　함께 내가 대화를 할 수 있는 지구 온난화에 대해

03 Perseus used a bright shield as a mirror **with which** he saw Medusa and cut off her head.

04 Posting comments on the Internet is an act **for which** people should be held responsible.

05 Tunnels are made to provide the soil with passageways **through which** air and water can circulate.

06 Elections can be a useful yardstick by which democratic development is measured.

07 The bigger the market is, the more people there are out there to whom you can sell your product.

08 They were given an hour's break during which time some were allowed to nap, while others had to stay awake.

09 Few books for traveling are better than a collection of poetry in which every page contains something complete.

10 You have at hand many examples of good characters from whom you will have learned the lessons by which you can live your own lives.

11 As I chose to ignore the compelling sign, a police car slowly approached, inside of which two police officers were watching me closely.

Part 4 소유격 whose (앞에 있는 명사의 소유격)

* whose는 앞에 있는 명사의 소유격으로 대신 사용하며, **사람, 사물** 둘 다에 사용된다.
of which the + 명사는 사물에만 사용되며, 현대 영어에서는 거의 사용되지 않는다.

01 I know the man **whose** house looks like a castle.(his)
나는 안다   남자를 그의 집이 성처럼 보이는
                        성처럼 보이는 집을 가진 남자를

02 I checked the car **whose** engine makes a strange noise.(its)
                    (whose는 사람, 사물 둘 다 사용가능)

03 She made the cake **of which the** smell was fantastic.
                        사물인 경우에는 항상 of which the

04 A woman **whose** husband has died is called a widow.
            남편이 죽은 여자를 미망인이라고 불려진다.

05 I found a man **whose extraordinary talent** can surprise people.

06 We will only accept an applicant **whose** degree is in politics.

07 The man whose income is less than his best friend **is eager** to get a better job.

08 **Babies** whose (=their) parents rarely talk to them or hold them **can be damaged** for life.

09 Jurors, **whose** identities will be kept secret, will be paid $40 a day.

10 Children **whose** parents **have emphasized** achievement over exploration tend to do things they do well.

11 The animal which has the widest frequency range is dolphins **whose** maximum frequency is three times as much as that of dogs.

12 The classes help her to increase her regular customers **whose** needs she must constantly meet.

Part 5 계속적 : 앞에 명사를 보충설명 하거나, 앞 문장을 가리키는 경우

*관계사 앞에 ,가 나오면 앞에 나온 명사를 가리켜 보충 설명하는 경우와 앞에 문장 전체를 가리키는 것에 사용하며, 접속사는 and, but, for등 다수가 있지만 대부분 and를 사용한다.

01 Your toaster, = **which** I bought only three weeks ago, doesn't work. (앞에 나온 명사와 동격)
너의 토스터기,　　　　　내가 단지 3주 전에 샀는데,　　　　작동이 안 된다.

02 Immortality, **which** means living forever, has been an unreachable ambition for many people.
불멸은,　=　영원히 사는 것을 의미하는데　　도달할 수 없는 야망 이었다　　많은 사람들에게

03 She visited the Empire State Building, **which** is in the center of New York City. (앞 단어 보충설명)
그녀는 Empire State Building를 방문했는데,　　[and it] 그리고 그것은 뉴욕의 중심에 있다.

04 This is my brother John, **whom** our whole family financially depend on. (John에 대한 보충설명)
이 애가 나의 brother 존인데,　[and him] 그리고 그에게 우리의 전 가족이 재정적으로 의존한다.

05 He said his mom stays healthy, **which** is a lie. (앞 문장 전체를 가리킴)
그는 그의 엄마가 건강하다고 말했다,　and it (그리고 그것은 거짓말 이다)

06 Bats use a unique low frequency, **which** can only be heard by allies. (= and it)

07 My son, Sean, had a talent for art, **which** he studied from childhood on. (= and it)

08 One of the boys kept laughing, **which** annoyed Jane intensely.

09 The house, which was completed in 1856, was famous for its huge marble gate.

10 Sir James, whose birthday is on February 26, plans to lay on a big party.

11 Desperate for money, she called her sister, whom she hadn't spoken to in 20 years.

12 Everybody worked really hard and helped tidy up at the end, which I hadn't expected at all.

13 More and more students might show a tendency to break the rules at school, which can lead to a classroom crisis.

14 Raw beans contain a certain acid, which is poisonous and can cause sickness and blood pressure problems.

15 Adequate hydration may improve cognitive function among children and adolescents, which is important for learning.

16 Big refrigerators encourage people to buy huge amounts of groceries just a few times a month, which results in the growth of supermarkets and destroys local grocery stores.

17 We human beings have the immune system, which enables the body to resist disease and recover more quickly from illness.

18 The Latin influence on American culture, which began with the earliest explorers and continues today, has become part of the cultural pattern of America.

19 Caffeine is a *diuretic, which means that you lose more water when drinking coffee than you gain by drinking it. (이뇨의)

20 Being financially stable, which means being financially independent of their own parents, ensures that their relationship with their partner will also be more secure.

21 Women are not allowed to play an important role in society, which means half of the knowledge, talent and strength that could improve conditions is literally going to waste.

Part 6. 수를 나타내는 of 관계대명사

* _____ of 관계사인 형태에서 앞에 사람이 나오는 경우 주격이라도 **whom**만 사용할 수 있다.

01 I have twelve co-workers, **most of whom** are British.
I have twelve co-workers, **and most of them** are British.
I have twelve co-workers, most of them are British. (X 시험에 자주 등장)

02 She bought a few paintings from an art collector, **one of which** turned out to be fake.

03 There are several schools around here, **some of which** are girls' schools.

04 Mike showed me a couple of bowling bowls, **neither of which** I liked to buy.

05 There are many adventures in the world, **not all of which** involve climbing mountains.

06 Logic has an extensive and well-defined set of rules and guidelines, **many of which** are all too easy to unintentionally violate.

Part 7. 관계사에 삽입 절이 들어 있는 경우 [주격]

01 I picked out some flowers **which** were most beautiful.
I picked out some flowers **which I believed** were most beautiful. (내가 믿기에)

02 What **you believe** is right may be wrong.

03 That is Mr. Johnson who **they say** is the most reliable man in the village. (whom은 사용 못함)

04 There are some places in nature that **just about everyone agrees** are amazing.

05 The boy whom **I thought** was selfish does voluntary work for our community every weekend. (X)

06 He was able to reach the kinds of students who **he believed** would make a difference in the world.

Part 8 관계부사

*관계부사는 부사 대신 사용하며 **관계부사 다음에 따르는 문장이 해석이 되고** 전치사+관계대명사로 바꿔 사용할 수 있다, **where를 제외하고는 둘 중에 하나는 생략할 수 있고**, 해석도 하나만 한다.

01 This is the castle **where our kings used to reside**. (뒤에 따르는 문장이 해석이 된다)
우리의 왕들이 거주 했었다 (where = there = in which)

02 **The reason why** they can't resolve conflict is that they don't listen to each other.
그들이 갈등을 해결 할 수 없는 이유는   그들이 서로의 말을 듣지 않아서이다.

03 Yesterday was **a day when** everything went wrong.
어제는 날 이였다 (때였다)   모든 것이 잘못 돌아갔던

04 **How** she treated her patients influenced a lot on would-be doctors. (the way, how는 같이 사용 못함)
그녀가 그녀의 환자를 다루는 방식은   많은 영향을 미쳤다 의사가 되려는 사람들에게

05 We might live in a world **where** paper is not an essential part of our lives.

06 Jail is a building **where** criminals are forced to live as a punishment.

07 Appearance can impact **the way** people perceive you, treat you and determine a promotion.

08 What is the reason why some organism do not produce the best molecules?

09 There will be a time when most students get accustomed to what they are doing.

10 There are a number of sites where military nuclear material is stored.

11 By the time you reach 40, the way you look shows what your life has been like.

12 Northern China is where high-speed winds and storms cause thick clouds of dry yellow dust.

Exercise 8

▶ 알맞은 것을 고르시오

01 Today is the day (when, which) she brings a cake.

02 Your birthday is today, (when, which) I never forget.

03 The library (where, which) she studies is quiet.

04 The library (where, which) he built is very quiet.

05 The reason (that, why) she was late was that she missed the train.

06 This is the way (how, that) he runs the company.

07 Seoul is the place (where, which) he meets people daily.

08 Seoul is the place (where, which) he always misses.

09 This is the castle (where, which) his father visits every year.

10 This is the oldest castle (where, which) the city will destroy next year for safety.

11 This is the moment (when, which) I will always remember.

12 The reason (how, why) she missed the bus was that she didn't know the exact schedule.

13 I'm trying to find out the way (how, that) she got to the destination.

14 This is the place (where, which) I hide my keys.

15 She told me to stay (which, where) I was.

❖ 해석하면서 자신의 것으로 만들기

01 The evolution which we have gone through is a piece of iceberg.

02 Scientists have wondered about body organs that don't seem to do anything useful.

03 The principle I keep is to show what kind of person I'm.

04 The Asian pupils I counseled complained of racial prejudice at the school.

05 All animals need their natural habitats where they can freely roam around.

06 The hypothesis, which I tested throughout the research, was rejected.

07 A man can succeed at almost anything for which he has unlimited enthusiasm.

08 True friendship is like sound health, the value of which is seldom known until it be lost.

09 Some scientists think of a desert as any region where the amount of moisture lost each year - mainly by evaporation - is more than *precipitation that falls. (강우량)

10 Sound is simply vibrating air which the ear picks up and converts to electrical signals, which are then interpreted by the brain.

11 Artificial light, which typically contains only a few wavelengths of light, do not seem to have the same effect on mood that sunlight has.

12 The procedure of an organ transplant is that a healthy organ is removed from somebody who has died and is transplanted into the person whose organ is not functioning properly.

❖ 중요한 것은 멈추지 않는 것

01 Every day one is faced with situations **which** are not what they appear. (제한적)

02 "Things Fall Apart", **which** is his first novel, is the most widely-read book in modern African literature.

03 Dogs, **which** can hear higher sounds than humans, can also hear higher sounds better than cats.

04 We cannot predict the outcomes of sporting contests, **which** vary from week to week. (계속적)

05 I know the author of this book, **who** has actually been to Turkey.

06 Stay at this beautiful hotel, **which** is close to one of the greatest national parks.

07 Newspaper is a cousin to paper towels, **which** were invented much later.

08 Some of my co-workers have to do a lot of paperwork, **which** is terribly boring.

09 Mike dug the ground to find something valuable, **which** proved to be useless.

10 He might rub his nose when it suddenly itches, **which** might give the other the impression that he is hiding something.

11 Dressing casually means employees act and think more freely. Then they will be more creative in work, **which** can lead to higher productivity.

12 Things that could be used in acts of violence are often found in students' lockers at school, **which** could be harmful to other students.

13 I met many experts in this field, **a few of whom** are from Britain.

14 There are many students studying in the library, **a third of whom** are girls.

15 Mike gave me a lot of pots, **most of which** I can't find at the market.

16 People gradually settled in parts of the continent **where** wild animals had roamed freely.

17 As the research suggests, most girls fall behind in physics and sciences **where** spatial ability is vital.

18 In any given situation **where** alternatives are available, a frightened person will inevitably anticipate the most negative situation.

19 Posco has spent around 300 million dollars on the AI project, **half of which** paid for the technology, design and equipment provided by Germany.

20 We should strengthen the immune system, **which** enables the body to resist disease and recover more quickly from illness.

21 We are often faced with high-level decisions, **where** we are unable to predict the results of those decisions.

22 The right to privacy may extend only to the point **where** it does not restrict someone else's right to freedom of expression or right to information.

23 One of the primary ways by **which** music is able to take on significance in our inner world is by the way it interacts with memory.

Chapter 7

Part 1. **비교급**

Part 2. **비교급인데 좀 다르네!!!**

Part 3. **원급 비교**

Part 4. **최상급**

Part 5. **비교급으로 최상급을**

Part 1 비교급

* 두 가지 대상 사이에서 어느 것이 더, 혹은 덜 하다는 우열 비교를 나타내는 표현이며
일반적으로 모음이 두 개 이상이면 more, 그렇지 않으면 ~er을 than과 더불어 사용한다.

01 She looks **more** attractive in black **than** in red.
　　그녀는 보인다 더 매력적으로　　검은색에서　빨간색보다

02 Children can absorb knowledge **much faster** than adults. (비교급 강조, even, still, far, a lot)
　　아이들은 지식을 흡수한다　　　훨씬 더 빨리　　성인들 보다

03 We have decided to take no **further** action against him. (far = farther, further)
　　우리는 더 이상의 조치를 취하지 않기로 결정했다 그에 대해

04 Workers **no longer** feel secure about the future. (더 이상 ~이 아닌)
　　노동자들은 더 이상 안전함을 느끼지 않습니다 미래에 대해

05 **Other than** her educational background, she qualifies for that position. (~을 제외하고)
　　　　　그녀의 학력 배경을 [제외하고]　　　　　그녀는 그 자리에 적격이야.

06 Many students want to be doctors to enjoy **higher** social status.

07 I told him to bring a **more** rational approach to dealing with problems.

08 Low fat milk contains much **fewer** calories than whole milk.

09 An image has a much greater impact on your brain than words.

10 Mammals tend to be **less colorful** than other animal groups.

11 Our research has resulted in a more profound appreciation of the problem.

12 Learn to breathe properly and you will benefit from a lower heart-rate, reduced blood pressure.

13 Experts say the definition of an addict has less to do with the number of hours spent online.

Part 2 비교급인데 좀 다르네!!!

A the more, the more (~할수록, 더 ~하다)
B more and more (점점 더)
C prefer A to B (B 보다 A를 더 선호하다)
D no more than (only)
E no less than (~나 되는, 다름 아닌)
F not less than (at least)
G would rather ~ than (~하기 보다는 차라리)

---

01 **The older** he grows, **the more** stubborn he gets. (~할수록 더욱 ~한)
그가 나이가 들수록 더욱 그는 완강해진다.

02 The outline of the ship became **more and more** distinct. (점점 ~더)
배의 윤곽이 점점 더 분명해진다.

03 A boy I know **prefers his imaginary world to reality**. (A to B: B보다 A를 선호한다)
                                 A   B

---

04 **The more limited** something is, **the more desired** it becomes.

05 Vast areas of rain forest disappear **faster** and **faster** every year.

06 Certainly it should be clear that **the more science** we possess, **the more** we need philosophy.

07 The more you are willing to do something, the more you are likely to achieve it.

08 Each box requires no more than a few hours of labor to build.

09 The higher the back of a chair, the greater the power of the person sitting in it.

10 By 1991, Britain was importing no less than 95% of its oil. (~나 되는)

11 We were standing **no more than** 10 yards away from the scene of the crime and we didn't realize it.

12 His life's mission is **no less than** to rescue the endangered creatures of the sea. (다름 아닌)

Part 3 원급 비교

*두 대상이 양이나 질에서 같은 것을 표현하며 as ~ as 사이에 변형 없는 형용사나 부사를 사용 하며 **앞의 as는 의미가 없고 뒤에 as만 ~만큼**이라고 해석. as 앞에 twice와 같은 배수가 나오면 일반 비교급의 의미가 되며, 부정어가 나오면 앞에 as를 so로 바꿔서 사용합니다.

---

01 Crying is as a primary emotion **as smiling**.
　　　　　　　　　　　　　　　　웃는 것만큼

02 This film is **as** instructive **as the book** I read last night.
　　　이 영화는　　　교육적이다　　책만큼　　내가 읽은 지난밤에

03 Sometimes they spread out in wide groups to catch **as many fish as possible**.
　　　　　　　　　　　　　　　　　　　　　　　　　　　가능한 많은 물고기를

---

04 Regular exercise is **as vital as** healthy food.

05 This hill is **as steep as** the one we climbed last week.

06 Somehow, Mike gets three times **as much wage as** his co-worker gets.

07 If you don't want to worry about being late for work, contact us as soon as possible.

08 Take notes as much as you can to help your better understanding of what you hear.

09 Our achievements once gained as much world attention as those of the first astronauts.

10 In 1980 the consumption of oil was far more than twice as much as that of Natural Gas.

11 As far as I know, she is more consistent in her actions. (~인 한)

12 It is just as important to keep wildlife from being too scarce as to stop them from being too plentiful.

13 Some experts estimate that as much as half of what we communicate is done through the way we move our bodies.

Part 4 최상급 (장소나 무리에서 가장 으뜸인 경우에 사용)

01 Emperor penguins are the largest **of** all the penguins.
황제 펭귄은   가장 크다   모든 펭귄 들 중에서

02 A snail is one of the most famous dishes **in** France.
가장 유명한 요리들 중의 하나

03 Seafood is the important source of high quality protein.
해산물은 가장 중요한 공급원이다.   고품질 단백질의

04 The new taxes were aimed at the largest and wealthiest corporations.
새로운 세금은 겨냥되어 진다.   가장 크고 가장 부유한 회사에

05 The latest attempt to reach a peace settlement ended in failure.
평화 정착에 이르려는 최신의 시도는   실패로 끝났다.

06 **The richest one percent** of the citizens own 40 percent of the total property of the country.

07 Bones are the parts of the body **least** sensitive to disease.

08 A country must import **at least** some professional manpower from other countries.

09 Last but not least, don't forget to turn the water off while you brush your teeth.

10 Watching sports was **by far** the most popular activity on Saturday afternoons. (최상급 강조 어구)

11 One of the most common strategies is not to move to the front early in the race and not to fall far behind.

12 Sugar has become the most commonly-used sweetener for altering the flavor and properties of food and drinks.

Part 5 비교급으로 최상급을 표현

01 **Nothing** is as valuable **as health** even though we disregard that fact.
　　　귀중한 것은 없다　　　　건강만큼　　　　비록 우리가 그 사실을 무시할지라도

02 **No other person** in competition is **more** aggressive **than her.**
　　　어느 다른 사람도 경쟁에 있어　　　　더 공격적이 않다　　그녀보다

03 He has never been **wealthier** than **ever before.**

04 Few people love you **more than** I do.

05 Health is **more valuable than any other thing** even though we disregard that fact.

06 No other animals presented in the chart have a lower heartbeat rate than humans.

07 Safe driving is more important than anything else.

08 Nothing is more attractive than a man who is fully committed to his woman.

09 Nothing is more precious than independence and freedom.

10 Nothing is as permanent as a temporary solution.

11 No one is more miserable than a person who does things from selfish ambition or from a cheap desire to boast.

12 Doing nothing is the worst thing that can happen. When you take action, you are sure to get results, and eventually you will get the results you desire.

CHECK POINT 19

❖ **해석을 통해 자신의 이해력 확인**

01 Meat is served only on special days, often not more than once a month.

02 I am more than happy to contribute some money to charity.

03 No other person in the group looks mature than David does.

04 Millions of years ago, human faces weren't as flat as they are today.

05 The older we get, the more we seem to fear falling down.

06 Failure is no more fatal than success is permanent.

07 Raising a child as adoptive parents is no less noble than being birth parents. (~ 못지 않은)

08 The two year ban which he received has been no more than a minor inconvenience to him.

09 The bigger the market is, the more people there are out there to whom you can sell your product.

10 Over the next 10 years in Africa, the epidemic is expected to kill more people and more children than all the wars of the 20th century combined.

11 You can make more friends in two months by becoming interested in other people than you can in two years by trying to get other people interested in you.

12 Apple vinegar breaks down your food into smaller pieces and the smaller the pieces are, the more efficiently you can absorb the nutrients.

13 Colleges expect students to try their best outside the classroom as well as accomplishments inside the classroom. (비교급 아님)

딱!
한권으로 정리되는
구문독해

Chapter 8

Part 1. **도치**

Part 2. **강조**

Part 3. **생략**

Part 4. **수의 일치**

Part 1 도치

*주어가 동사나, 조동사와 위치가 바뀌는 경우이며 대부분 강조하기 위해 사용합니다.

1) 문두에 부정어 Not, Never가 나오는 경우

01 **Not until** Friday **did I** find out someone took my book without my permission.

I did**n't** find out **until** Friday someone took my book without my permission.
금요일이 되고 나서야 비로소 나는 알았다 누가 나의 책을 가져갔는지 나의 허락 없이

02 I never saw such a strange animal.

Never did I see such a strange animal. (조동사가 없으면 만들어서 문장 구성)

03 Not only **will she** dance extraordinarily but also sing elegantly.

She will not only dance extraordinarily but also sing elegantly.

04 **No sooner had they** come back from a trip **than** they planned another one.

They **had come** back from a trip **no sooner than** they planned another one.(하자마자)

05 **Hardly a month goes by without** another factory closing down. (관용적인 표현)

06 Not until we lose our beloved ones, **do we realize** the value of them.

07 **Not only did** Susie start playing the piano before she could speak, but also could compose music at a very early age.

2) ~도 그러하다.

08 David was not at the meeting, **nor was** he at work yesterday.

09 Sam didn't believe a word she said, and **neither did** the police.

10 We human beings need nitrogen to live, **so do all living things**.

11 I have never told anyone about the accident before, **nor have** I tried to explain to myself why I haven't.

12 When I left for New York, I couldn't think of anything to say to my father and **neither could he**.

3) 장소부사가 나오는 경우 (주어+동사 위치만 바꾼다)

13 **At our feet lies** the valley. (우리의 발아래 계곡이 놓여있다)

14 **On a hill in front of us stood** a huge castle.

15 To his right were sitting the nuns who were going to pray.

16 Inside the shell are oyster's mouth, heart, stomach.

17 In the back seat of the car next to mine (was / were) two little sweet boys.

4) 일반 부사가 나오는 경우

18 **Only by shouting was he** able to show his fury.
= He was able to show his fury **only by shouting**.
단지 소리를 지름으로써, 그는 그의 분노를 보여 줄 수 있었다.

19 **So mature** is **she** that no one thinks of her as a child.

20 **Only after** everyone had finished lunch would the hostess inform her guests that what they had just eaten was neither tuna salad nor chicken salad but rather rattlesnake salad. (~하고 나서야 비로소)

5) 가정법에서 if가 생략되는 경우

21 **Were it not for** your help, she couldn't do it.
If it were not for your help, she couldn't do it. 너의 도움이 없다면, 그녀는 그것을 할 수 없을 텐데.

22 **Had it not been** for your help, she couldn't have done it.

23 Were it not for humans, woolly mammoths would have lived for 4,000 more years.

24 Had it not been for his mother, he would have remained imprisoned in his own world.

Part 2 강조

*주어가 동사나, 조동사와 위치가 바뀌는 경우이며 대부분 강조하기 위해 사용합니다.

1) It is ~ that: 주어, 목적어, 장소, 시간 부사구를 강조하기 위해 사용

Mike watched an action movie with Jenny last night.
= It was **Mike** that watched an action movie with Jenny last night.
= It was **an action** movie that Mike watched with Jenny last night.
= It was **with Jenny** that Mike watched an action movie last night.
= It was **last night** that Mike watched an action movie with Jenny.

2) do를 이용한 동사 강조 (do + 동사원형)

You don't like port, but I **do** like it a lot.
This soup **does** smell really fantastic.
John really **did** love Kevin, but she dumped him.

3) 부정문, 의문문 강조

(ever, on earth, in the world)

What **on earth** did you do that for? (도대체)
What **in the world** are you doing here at seven in the morning?
I do**n't** care where you want to go **at all**. (전혀 ~ 아닌)
The charm of this small Southern city **hardly ever** fails.

Part 3 생략

*주 문장에서 어구가 동일하게 반복되거나 혹은 없어도 의미 파악이 쉬운 경우에는 생략하여 문장을 간결하게 한다.

01 As (**it was**) planned, he did what he was supposed to do and got the good result.
  계획대로   그는 해야 할 일을 했고 좋은 결과를 얻었다.

02 When (**you are**) tempted to criticize your parents, spouse, or children, bite your tongue.
  부모님, 배우자, 자녀들을 비난하고 싶을 때 (유혹 받을 때),

03 They're closing this factory but (**they are**) building two new ones in another area.
  그들은 이 공장은 문을 닫는데   하지만 짓고 있어요   두 곳을 새로 다른 지역에.

04 We prepared a lot for the unexpected. **If not**, we would have died many times over by now.

05 Whether we like it or not, we are controlled by, rather than **in control of**, natural forces.

06 It is undesirable to express one's opinion **while hiding** one's identity.

07 She did everything she **could** to bring the best result.

08 Mammals on the whole are not melodious and there is little evidence that they intend to be.

09 Sustainable development is development which aims to protect, not destroy, the earth's resources.

10 The heart of all innovative conceptions lies in the borrowing from, adding to, or changing of an old idea.

11 When starting out, don't worry about not having enough money. Limited funds are a blessing, not a curse.

12 When I couldn't find the passports – honestly, I didn't know whether **to laugh** or cry!
                                                    I should laugh or cry!

Part 4 수의 일치

＊주어가 단수인지 복수인지에 따라 동사가 취하는 형태, 특히 단수인 경우가 시험에 많이 나오며
주어와 동사가 서로 멀리 떨어져 있는 경우 잘 파악해야 하며, 단수 취급하는 경우: each, every, either, neither
뒤에 나오는 주어에 동사가 정해지는 경우: most of, some of, not only A but also,

01 The most popular **event** at rodeos is bull riding.
   로데오에서 가장 인기 있는 종목은 황소타기에요.

02 An important **quality** of plastics is that they are easy to shape.
   플라스틱의 중요한 특성은 모양을 만들기 쉽다는 것입니다.

03 **One** of the most important things sports can do is (to) build self-esteem.

04 Around **fifty percent** of world's **population lives** close to the ocean.

05 **The number of** people he is going to meet today is limited to a few due to a busy schedule.

06 **A number of** people going to aborad to get a job (seems / seem) to feel frustrated.

07 Neither of the students (is / are) eager to participate in the contest.

08 **Most** of the candy industry's total **sales** of around $28 billion per year (is/are) sold around the holidays.

09 Practical activities that we perform every day, such as cleaning or getting dressed, (doesn't / don't) give us the physical enjoyment that we get from play.

10 Two communication devices that have come into common usage (is / are) the text message and voice mail.

11 The distinctive features between Korea's four beautiful seasons which have been a great pride for its people (is / are) becoming unclear.

❖ 마무리를 잘 해야지!!!

01 Little money did she save for herself.

02 Hardly did he fulfill one of his dreams.

03 Butterflies lay their eggs on a plant which the young, when hatched, will feed on.

04 If possible, I will contact John and ask him to deal with the problem.

05 Not until the rain stopped could we see the view of the ocean.

06 The problem would not have been resolved had it not been for our action.

07 Not only have prices gone up considerably, but also some are hard to get.

08 Only by travelling other countries can we come to understand uniqueness of different cultures.

09 No longer will Mike be for your sponsor in the future.

10 On the right side of my desk are file folders containing the main lectures I will be giving this year.

11 When asked whether they were illiterate, they suddenly kept silent.

12 Groundborne vibrations, if perceived, can serve as an early warning system.

13 When meeting someone for the first time, resist asking what they do for a living. Enjoy their company without attaching any labels.

14 The challenge for educators is to ensure individual competence in basic skills while adding learning opportunities that can enable students to also perform well in teams.

memo

memo